KINDRED SPIRITS

Artwork by Debra Whelan entitled "Kindred Spirits".

KINDRED SPIRITS

Michael Grgich
and
Suzanne Newman

Accompanying Artwork
by Debra Whelan

RESOURCE *Publications* • Eugene, Oregon

KINDRED SPIRITS

Copyright © 2022 Suzanne Newman, Michael Grgich, and Debra Whelan. All rights reserved. Except for brief quotations in critical publications or reviews, no part of this book may be reproduced in any manner without prior written permission from the publisher. Write: Permissions, Wipf and Stock Publishers, 199 W. 8th Ave., Suite 3, Eugene, OR 97401.

Resource Publications
An Imprint of Wipf and Stock Publishers
199 W. 8th Ave., Suite 3
Eugene, OR 97401

www.wipfandstock.com

PAPERBACK ISBN: 978-1-6667-3679-3
HARDCOVER ISBN: 978-1-6667-9560-8
EBOOK ISBN: 978-1-6667-9561-5

FEBRUARY 11, 2022 10:40 AM

Contents

Preface | ix

KINDRED SPIRITS – PART ONE

Louder* | 3
Untouchable Soul | 5
Succour's Bus | 7
The Devil's Rose * | 8
Obstacle | 11
Restored | 13
Staircase * | 16
Trials Comes Knocking | 20
Clinging | 23
Glint * | 25
Christians Suffer Too | 28
I Don't Know Much | 29
Baggage * | 31
Because Of The Light | 33
Post-Cancer's Stormy Seas | 35
The Light At The End Of The Tunnel * | 37
Bouncer | 40

Battle Scars | 43
Pointless (Satan's Halo) * | 44
The Fortress Inside Me | 47
An Everyday Pilgrim | 48
Hope In The Darkest Of Places * | 50
Sanctuary | 53
Nothing Can Outshine The Lord | 54
Caged * | 56
Moving House | 59
Broken Pottery | 61
I'm Not A Sun Worshipper, But I Am A Son Worshipper! * | 62
Naked Before God | 64
Thief | 66
Ablaze | 68
Hanging By A Thread * | 70
Playground | 72

KINDRED SPIRITS —PART TWO

Welcome To My Mind | 77
Heathen To Heaven * | 78
Quicksand | 81
Two Equals One | 82
Depths * | 84
Satan's Throne | 86
Broken Wings | 89
Chain Of Life * | 90
God's Pinocchio | 93

Lost | 94

The Cross * | 95

Battle For Eternity | 97

Cracked | 101

Pray Tm (Pray To Me) * | 102

The Afternow | 105

Paradise | 106

The Dark * | 107

Freight Train | 109

In The Mirror | 110

Blessings * | 112

The Storm | 114

Broken Road | 115

Wings | 116

Waterfall * | 117

The Voice | 119

Dig | 121

Release * | 122

Seven Nails | 124

A Tired Old Man | 126

The Call | 128

You Heal Me * | 129

My Day Of Judgement | 131

Personal Testimonies | 133

Personal Testimonies | 135

Personal Testimonies | 138

Steps | 141

PREFACE

WE'RE SO THRILLED TO bring you "Kindred Spirits"- a collection of faith-based poetry that expresses our abundant love, devotion and praise for our amazing Father God.

The three of us . . . Michael Grgich, Debra Whelan and Suzanne Newman, have joined forces to share the depth of our hearts and souls through our words and imagery. Life is such an incredible gift, but the truth is it's not always a smooth, easy-going journey. It is defined as much by the unavoidable, inevitable hardships and upsets, as it is by the joys and triumphs we all encounter throughout our time here on earth.

As we experience trials and struggles, God begins to refine, mature and mould us, much in the same way as a blacksmith does when he forges a molten piece of iron in the fire! When the metal is subjected to intense heat, it becomes pliable and mouldable. As the heat intensifies, it begins to glow as the blacksmith files, hammers and twists it into a more usable, suitable shape, fit for purpose. God loves us so much that He uses trials and tribulations to accomplish a similar transformation in His children. As we grow in our faith, we become wiser and better equipped to face whatever may challenge us next.

The primary purpose of this book is to celebrate and share the grace and glory of our Divine God. Its messages are meant to provide inspiration, strength, encouragement, and the hope that is always found within true spiritual peace. In a troubled world filled with uncertainty, the one constant is our ever-loving, Sovereign God, whose Covenant promises can always be relied upon to bring hope and comfort all who trust in Him and believe in Jesus Christ as our Lord and Savior. Our goal with this book, is to inspire and encourage you into cultivating a deeper, more intimate spirit-filled relationship with our loving Father and we pray that you receive eternal and abundant blessing by His transformative light and life.

Preface

Thank you for buying this book and we hope you enjoy it. We acknowledge that we are just three humble sinners, saved in grace through The Lord Jesus Christ. Without Him we are nothing and with Him, anything is possible!

We ourselves cannot save you . . . only your faith and want to find and embrace our Lord Jesus Christ can do that. However, through the book "Kindred Spirits" we at least hope to humbly offer you a road map to start to find Him, by witnessing to His greatest and faithfulness during times of personal struggle. Much love, and may God bless you all.

ALL GLORY TO GOD . . . ALWAYS.

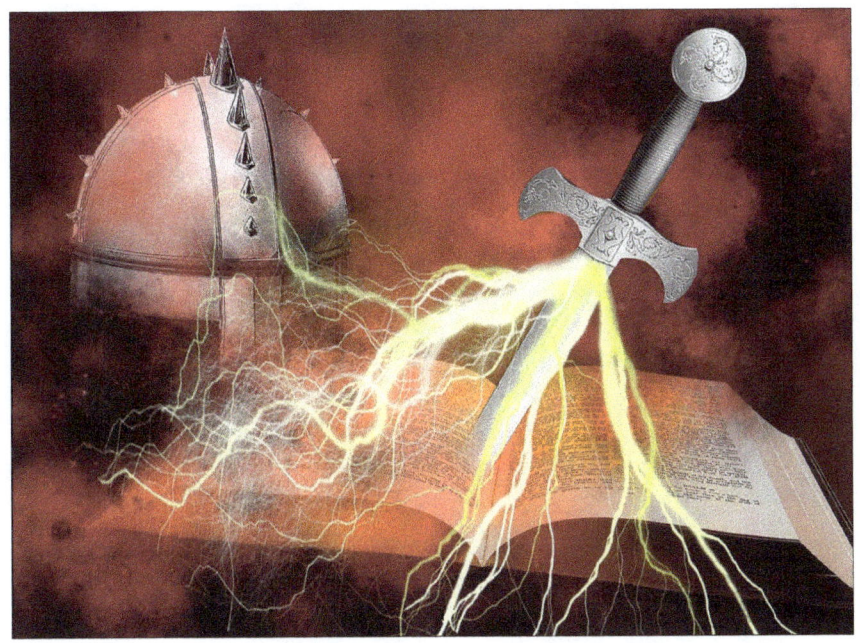

Artwork by Debra Whelan entitled "God's Armor".

KINDRED SPIRITS – PART ONE

ALL POEMS WRITTEN BY SUZANNE NEWMAN

ARTWORK BY DEBRA WHELAN

(All rights reserved)

CONTENTS – (* = ACCOMPANIED BY ARTWORK)

1 - LOUDER *
2 – UNTOUCHABLE SOUL
3 – SUCCOUR'S BUS
4 – THE DEVIL'S ROSE *
5 – OBSTACLE
6 – RESTORED
7 – STAIRCASE *
8 – TRIALS COMES KNOCKING
9 – CLINGING
10 – GLINT *
11 – CHRISTIANS SUFFER TOO
12 – I DON'T KNOW MUCH
13 – BAGGAGE *
14 – BECAUSE OF THE LIGHT
15 – POST CANCER'S STORMY SEAS
16 – THE LIGHT AT THE END OF THE TUNNEL *
17 – BOUNCER
18 – BATTLE SCARS
19 – POINTLESS (Satan's halo) *
20 – THE FORTRESS INSIDE ME
21 – AN EVERYDAY PILGRIM
22 – HOPE IN THE DARKEST OF PLACES *
23 – SANCTUARY
24 – NOTHING CAN OUTSHINE THE LORD
25 – CAGED *
26 – MOVING HOUSE
27 – BROKEN POTTERY
28 – I'M NOT A SUN WORSHIPPER, BUT I AM A SON WORSHIPPER! *
29 – NAKED BEFORE GOD
30 – THIEF
31 – ABLAZE
32 – HANGING BY A THREAD *

LOUDER*

I'm louder than the roaring tides that crash around my head,
I'm louder than depression's lies that permeate & want me dead,
Louder than the lightning cracks that whip to strike me down,
And louder than The Devil's shouts which echo all around.

I'm louder than my stress's screams, which sound like a pneumatic drill,
I'm louder than hyena's laughs, as they circle in & move to kill,
Louder than the storms of life which hurl & clatter debris,
And louder than the vultures, who have come to pick the flesh off me.

I'm louder than past's earthquake, which builds up to shake me down,
I'm louder than pain's avalanche, whose blanket pins me to the ground,
Louder than a lion's roar, a jet engine or falling tree,
And louder than frustration's yells, which wail just like a hurt banshee.

I'm louder than all of this noise, for my saved soul is strong,
My faith in God unshakeable, my length of love for Him too long,
My heart still sings His praises in the middle of this tempest,
And I shout all my troubles down, for I know His Grace does leave me blessed.

And as I cry out happily, it rocks the very gates of Hell,
I know I can't be swept away by swirling winds or killer swells,
And angels up in Heaven all join in to make the praises rise,
Up to The Lord, creator & sustainer of the earth & skies.

And nothing is more powerful than God, so as His precious child,
I call upon His Holy roar to quash the din, however wild,
Emboldened in His awesome might, secure within His love & care,
I know I won't be broken, despite the troubles that do rage & tear.

For I am standing firm upon the rock of God, The Cornerstone,
And keep my thoughts & eyes & ears focused upon my spirit's home,
So I can weather stormy skies, life's trials & The Devil's schemes,
As God gives me the voice to overpower it all & supersede.

Artwork for the poem
"Louder".

UNTOUCHABLE SOUL

It's a predatory carnivore, sticky black leech,
A vampiric creature that's caustic like bleach,
It wants to consume me and swallow me whole,
It's after my essence, mind, body and soul.

It paralyses like a painkilling drug,
It's merciless, brutal, like a jail-hardened thug,
It keeps pressing forward, this ravenous beast,
For it can't get enough of my mind for its feast.

And, once it has hollowed-out much of my brain,
Refilled it with lead, tried to drive me insane,
It hauls its fat entity further inside,
To seek out my soul, despite my pitied cries.

I feel its cold fingers and foul breath draw near,
I sense my heart panic and flutter with fear,
But just as depression is nearing my middle,
And licking its lips, with fangs dripping in dribble,

It's forced to a halt, and can go on no further -
There's a barrier here which is guarded by fervour!
My love for The Lord is too deep and unshakable,
Our Holy bond holds, forever unbreakable.

Depression's dark beast has to stop in its tracks,
For God's light from my soul is now hurting it's black,
Its eyes forced to close, and it winces in pain,
It can't touch my soul, 'though it reaches and strains.

For my soul is owned by The Lord God above,
And protected by Him, in Grace, mercy and love,
And nothing on earth can pierce, hurt or harm it,
For He'll over-power, destroy and disarm it.

So, my soul is strong in God's promise and power,
'though depression does torment, and pace, snarl and glower,
It won't hurt me further and can't make me yield,
When I have The Lord as my fortress and shield.

SUCCOUR'S BUS

This road of struggles seems so long, as I trudge on my own,
It goes over the horizon, and I'm tired and all alone,
The landscape's looking sparse and dry, I'm zapped by the sun's heat,
My shoes are worn and tattered and I've blisters on my feet.

My posture's getting much more slumped, sweat hangs off me in drops,
Just when I think I will collapse a bus pulls up and stops.
The automated-door folds back and inside there's a man,
Who's smiling at me kindly and holds out a loving hand.

He says that I can climb aboard so I can rest my head,
That there are many others here, who share this road I tread,
"But I've no money" I admit, "I can't travel for free!",
"Of course you can", the man replies, "Through faith and trust in me".

I look closer and am stunned to see it is The Lord who speaks!
He's not left me to walk alone and knows I'm strained and weak,
"I heard your heart call out to me, I listened to each prayer,
I'm here to be your loving crutch and give you Grace and care.

For "Succour" is my bus's name, I'm guide and navigator,
Wise counsellor and driver, trusted friend and motivator,
You have a place reserved on here through MY name, Grace and blood,
And it does provide you shelter, from the storms and heat and floods.

So, step onboard my valued child and let me take your load,
Together we will travel-on along this bumpy road,
You'll find your siblings on this bus, who also share your trial,
They love you in my precious name and will sit and chat a while!"

So Jesus helps me up the steps and shows me to my place,
I'm humbled to know in HIS strength, I'm able to complete the race;
I'm happy beyond measure to let Jesus take the lead,
And trust Him in my journey, for whatever I may need.

THE DEVIL'S ROSE *

This red rose sure looks beautiful,
My eyes transfix on it,
Distracted and lured by its beauty,
And the way that its full petals sit.

The colour is vibrant crimson,
Dew hangs on the petals like jewels,
Looking flawless this time of the morning,
As the sun catches it in light-pools.

I move closer in order to smell it,
And to marvel a little bit more,
I forget other things I was doing,
Was I going this way? I'm not sure.

As I reach my hand out to cup the rose,
I see that its beauty's skin-deep,
For lurking beneath the lush foliage,
Is a stem that has thorns just like teeth.

An angry bee's trapped in the flower,
The light round the bush is now dim,
From afar this vision seemed gorgeous,
But now close-up I see it's just grim.

My arm becomes scratched and my hand starts to bleed
Where the thorns are attacking my skin,
I discover this rose has no fragrance,
And holds nothing attractive within.

I withdraw my limb from this enticing trap,
And head back to the path in the light,
Never again will I be so duped,
Nor be harmed by its deceptive sight.

So, now I am wary, suspicious, alert,
If a tempting sight catches my eye,
I'll continue along on the right path ahead,
I won't stop and will just walk on by.

Artwork for the poem
"The Devil's Rose".

OBSTACLE

Why have you placed this before me Lord?
And why is it blocking my way?
Why have you asked me to push it so hard,
From dawn until dusk every day?

It's too tall for me to climb over Lord,
It's too wide for me to squeeze past,
I don't know just how I can move this,
When its size is too weighty and vast.

But I know that it needs to be moved Lord,
As I cannot get past it to go,
Further down on this path I must travel,
And my stress is now starting to grow.

No matter how long I keep trying,
How hard that I push, heave or tug,
I really can't make this obstacle move
Just an inch, for it won't even budge!

I want to give up Lord, I can't see the point,
When I know I am getting nowhere,
I don't know what more I can do Lord,
For whatever I try, it's still there.

So I pray up to Heaven to you Lord,
Where you hear my pitiful pleas,
Although I fear that I have failed you,
You still smile at me and are pleased!

For you didn't expect me to move it all,
And this never was part of your plan!
You know I'm unable to shift it,
And I have all the weakness of man.

You tell me that moving this obstacle,
Was not what you expected or asked,
What you wanted to see was persistence,
And in this sense, I have done the task!

For 'though I was not making progress,
I still bowed my head and obeyed,
To just keep on pushing this object,
From dawn until dusk every day.

The point of this all was to exercise trust
In you, so it would help me grow,
You need me to persevere in my faith,
My prayers and obedience so . . .

I hone and develop relations with you,
Become better equipped and feel strong,
In order that I am now better prepared,
For whatever does next come along.

For this won't be the last of my hurdles,
And life is one big learning-curve,
But still you do love me and aid me in Grace,
Which I know is more than I deserve.

So I'll exercise trust and obedience,
At whatever you set me to do,
When an obstacle for me is immovable,
I must wait and just trust in you.

For I know that you're Holy and mighty and wise,
And when the time's right I shall see,
That YOU will remove any obstacle,
And that strength comes from you and not me!

RESTORED

In a darkened alley, damp and black,
Is a broken doll, neglected and cracked,
Her floppy limbs are lacking strength,
Once fine glossy hair now just tangled lengths.

She's lying helpless, weak, forlorn,
Far from the light and warmth of dawn,
She longs to have a happy home,
Somewhere she's loved and call her own.

But she's currently out in the cold,
Where suffering's made her frail and old,
She can't recall when she was new,
With perfect paint and dress ice-blue.

For now, she's just all torn and tattered,
Out in the rain and weather-battered,
Unloved, unwanted, tired and low,
She has no other place to go.

She fears that she'll just rot away,
Fade into nothing in the dreary grey,
She feels there's nothing to fight for,
And her tear-stained eyes are bloodshot sore.

But just when she thinks hope has gone,
She hears a voice that's kind and strong,
Someone is offering to take
Her pain away and mend her breaks.

They say they'll stitch her worn-out seams,
Redress her, make her nice and clean,
Touch up her paint and find her shoes,
Provide her with a new home too.

She's glad but doesn't understand,
Why this person lends a helping hand,
How is it that they see her worth,
When she's lost and broken in the dirt?

But then things don't seem quite as odd,
When she sees this man is The Son of God!
For Jesus Christ has come to seek,
All broken souls and save the meek.

And in His Grace we all can share
In Heaven's peace, find our home there,
For by His blood we become paired,
And are justified, safe, in His care.

So Jesus Christ, Lord, king of kings,
Master-craftsman does gently bring
This broken doll in to His care,
To be renewed, restored, repaired.

For He's full of mercy, compassion, Grace,
And never shuns or hides His face,
From those who cry out to be saved,
And He'll reclaim all those who've strayed.

And not through anything we've done,
But because He's awesome, God The Son,
And He fought sin and death and won,
Stands conqueror over all – it's done!

And so this doll knows she is blessed,
That she can wear Christ's righteousness,
Is comforted when she is stressed,
To know she puts on armoured dress.

And, just as promised, Christ does mend
All that is broken, for He's Lord yet friend,
With a love that never fades or ends,

Won't wax or wane like earthly trends.

And so this doll's renewed, restored,
Filled with The Spirit in Grace out-poured,
Better than before, she'll never get bored,
Of singing all praises to Christ The Lord!

STAIRCASE *

I'm standing on a staircase,
Which is long with many bends,
I'm waiting in the middle as I
Can't see either end.
When I look up, towards the top,
I see a blurry light,
In contrast, when I look below,
There's darkness like the night.

To go upwards looks effort,
For it does seem quite a climb,
While the way down looks far easier
And I'll get there in no time.
The upwards stairs seem daunting –
Steep, with wood that looks quite old,
I see a few uneven parts,
But there's a handrail I can hold.

The down-stairs look much wider,
And on each step is a treat!
There's a welcome sign in red lights,
And warm carpet for my feet!
The way up looks quite simple,
But I see few people go,
There's a huge queue for the other way-
On the stairs that lead below.

There's nervous looks and chatter.
Anticipation's in the air;
When everyone starts guessing,
What is down the broader stairs.
The way up's far more reverent,
But the climbers still seem pleased,
As they know what's waiting for them there,

Which puts them all at ease.

On the down-stairs there are ushers,
In red suits, on every bend,
With polished smiles and velvet gloves,
Who vow the fun won't end!
The ascending steps have just one guide,
Who helps those travelling up,
They trust in all His promises,
And drink from His Holy cup.

The ushers on the down-stairs
Offer all kinds of nice things,
Like fine wine, cash and lovers,
Treat the queuers just like kings!
On the up stairs there is just one king,
That people all bow to,
And because they love and trust in Him,
They'll share His Heavenly view.

But the self-reliant travellers,
Upon the downward stairs,
All think that they know better
As they dance without a care.
It looks like one big party,
In some hedonistic club,
'though no-one's truly happy,
For it's lacking any love.

As I peer closer at the top,
I know the pure light's peace,
I sense there's love and mercy,
And all pain and worries cease.
Then I see the fine façade slip-off,
Upon the downward stairs,
For the ushers are all demons,
And unhappiness lurks there.

They lure you in with niceties,
And tempt with all life's pleasures,
But when the devil owns your soul,
You just hold hollow treasures.
I see now that life's true rewards
Are Spiritual in form,
For all God's gifts are precious,
And keep our souls safe and warm.

So I will choose the up-stairs,
Pray for those who're on the down,
And know one day through Jesus' blood,
I'll receive my Heavenly crown.
All will be well; I'll rest in peace,
While the "downers" get a shock,
For life in Hell's no fun at all,
Where the light of God's been blocked.

Artwork for the poem
"Staircase".

TRIALS COMES KNOCKING

I'm sitting comfy on the couch,
Feel quite relaxed and calm, assured,
When suddenly there's rapping, banging,
Knocking, hard, on my front door.

I'm caught off-guard and startled,
Rise, in panic, rush towards to see,
What's making this disturbance,
Which has worried and unsettled me.

"Good Evening Ma'am" a grim voice says,
"My name is 'Trials', I've come to call".
My stomach churns in terror,
For I've heard this many times before.

This figure looms before me -
A Goliath of a man, in black,
Who holds a stick to beat me with,
And sneers and winks, then tips his hat.

His teeth are brown and rotten,
And his skin's a deathly, whitened hue,
His eyes are black, like pinholes,
For inside them he holds sorrow's view.

His shout does rage like thunder
And booms loud enough to shake the ground,
Trial's constant nagging claws the mind,
And makes my temples ache and pound.

His overcoat swings slowly
In the troubled winds of change he brings,
He holds a cloth to smother
Any happiness or hymns I sing.

And by his feet there sits a sack,
In which he plans to capture hope,
Trials thoroughly enjoys his work,
And loves to see me fret and mope.

And laughing, just behind him,
I spy Satan, who has come to prance,
And relish in my struggles
That this latest test will make me dance.

Then Trials beckons me outside,
With cruel, cold finger, sickly smile,
I feel sad, apprehensive,
And my heart thumps, frantic all the while.

But as I step to go with Trials,
I find that I don't walk alone,
For Jesus Christ stands with me,
And I'm backed-up by His Heaven's throne!

The Father hears my prayers and pleas,
Gifts courage and strength in His grace,
The Spirit, deep inside me,
Makes me roar and stare in Trial's face.

Christ Jesus holds my trembling hand,
And whispers "Do not be afraid",
So then I feel emboldened,
Not so scared of Trial's troubled-shade.

The Devil ceases laughing,
Trial's cocky smile drops to a frown,
When they realize that they can't defeat
A co-heir of Christ's righteous crown.

Then Jesus and I stride on out,
Along the route that Trials has planned,
I'm confident I'll see it through,

For I'm upheld by God's great hand.

Trials does his best to trip me up,
I stumble, but won't ever fall,
For I'm carried and helped along,
Whilst guided by The Shepherd's call.

CLINGING

Here I am, clinging onto my God, my hope,
Like a clump of furry moss
Clinging on to a damp stone in a babbling brook,
Or the last crimson leaf refusing to fall from a tree
Swaying in the Autumn gusts.

I'm a seahorse, wrapping its tail around coral
To anchor itself to avoid getting swept away
By the strong ocean currents that surge.

I'm a child's toy windmill,
Frantically spinning in a gale,
But whilst its sails may become tattered
As it is buffeted by the storms,
It stays standing, as its pole is firmly rooted in good soil.

I am like lichen clinging on to a fallen branch in a dark wood,
Fungi hanging in soft white shelves off a tree-trunk
Which grows defiantly against the odds!
I am a limpet welded on to a slippery rock on the shoreline,
Determined, immoveable,
Despite the constant pounding of the stinging waves on my side.
I am a baby Koala,
Firmly nestled on my loving parent's back
Where I am safe, nurtured, and protected against predators.

I am a snowflake clinging on to the mountain top,
Vulnerable as the glare of the sun tries to melt me,
The icy storms try to blow me away,
And avalanches try to shake and dislodge me
To send me hurtling down the rocky slope
To be crushed at the bottom.

But I continue to cling to the mountain top
With all my might,

For it is my God –
My rock and my Salvation.

You may say I'm weak,
Clinging on to God like this as I do,
But it takes strength, persistence and courage to cling on,
To stay firm,
Unshakable and defiant against the harsh elements.
And I am not a lone snowflake on this mountain,
For there are millions of us,
All combining
To make a pure, soft snowy-white blanket,
Shining out brightly in all its splendour
For everyone to see its quiet, calm, secure and serene beauty,
Reflected in The Lord's Heavenly light and power.

I am not ashamed to admit I am clinging on,
For God does not view me as weak for this,
But rather,
Faithful.
For it takes a determined strength of faith,
And a stubborn hope and trust
To cling on to a ledge by your fingertips,
And not allow yourself to fall.

GLINT *

There's a fiendish glint in The Devil's eyes,
When not far off he thinks he spies
A line of tasty mortal souls,
Which he plans to eat and swallow whole.
But as he starts to prowl and pace,
And salivates, grin on his face,
The nearer he gets to this line,
The clearer he sees what's behind.

The Devil's happy glinting eyes,
Turn sour and soon begin to cry,
As he can see The Lord stands there
Behind this line, that's not laid bare.
For these souls aren't the easy picking
The Devil thought, not finger-licking,
For they're the army of The Lord,
Stand undeterred and faithful, sure.

And now the glint's seen in God's eyes,
For His Holy will can't be denied,
He's lined His soldiers up to fight,
And gifts to each His Holy might.
And in the sunset's pinky hues,
The Devil shudders at the view,
Of many shining armoured souls,
Strong in The Lord, glinting like gold.

And as The Devil casts an eye,
Across this army standing by,
He sees each helmet has beneath,
Fierce glinting eyes and smiling teeth;
For Earth's got nothing to compare
To the light of God, and the power that's there,
His soldiers stand assured and still,
More than equipped to do His will.

Now The Devil's glint has shrivelled, died,
He hurries off, just slinks on by,
Near-blinded as he's forced to turn,
From the Holy light that glares and burns.
The glinting armour of this line,
Stays impenetrable through sin and time,
And nothing matches or beats God's glint,
So The Devil leaves, for he takes the hint!

Artwork for the poem
"Glint".

CHRISTIANS SUFFER TOO

"I just need to forewarn you, my precious one,
I know you've been saved in my Grace through The Son,
But that doesn't mean your life will be all rosy,
All comfortable, happy, content, nice and cosy,
For there will be trying times for you ahead,
Times when you'll be panicked and filled up with dread,
Times when you'll be tempted to stray from my road,
Times when you'll feel weary, lugging life's painful load.

There'll be times when you're angry and sad or confused,
Times when you're let-down, attacked, persecuted, abused,
Times when you will grieve for a dear loved-one lost,
Times when you'll lose focus of Christ on the cross,
Times you'll be in pain and have huge scars that show,
But throughout all these times, my dear child, please do know,
That I'll NEVER leave you to struggle alone,
And will hear ALL your prayers from my Heavenly throne.

I'll comfort and shepherd, remind you you're loved,
By The Lord, your creator and sustainer above,
I've plans to uphold you and teach you in trials,
And I'll be your support and let you rest a while,
I'll help you to learn the things you have to know,
In order to be wise, get stronger and grow,
You need to mature so your faith gets to work,
And I'm sorry, but to do this, it IS gonna hurt.

But, keep trusting in me and I won't let you down,
Then in Glory I'll grant you eternal life's crown,
I'll smile at you as you come through Heaven's gate,
"Welcome in, faithful servant; I am pleased. You did great!"
For faith in good times isn't hard or a chore,
It's only fully tested through the fire at Hell's door,
But I WILL keep you strong, won't let go of your hand,
I'll be all that you need, so in each trial, you'll stand."

I DON'T KNOW MUCH

I don't know that much now, Dementia has got me,
It robbed me at gun point & now it's just shot me,
I don't know how to dress, brush my teeth or eat,
My brain's a dark maze where I feel lost & beat.

I don't know the names of my loved-ones who visit,
Can't recognise old friends, or neighbours – who is it?
Don't know what the time is, nor day of the week,
My mind aches with loss & feels so cold & bleak.

But one thing I DO know, is that God still loves me,
I still have redemption & Heaven's above me,
I still feel The Spirit that Christ sent to dwell,
In me, years ago, so I won't go to Hell.

For nothing has changed in me Salvation-wise,
For Jesus still looks on me with loving eyes,
And I still love God, 'though my brain's weak & sore,
I know my soul's safe, well, at peace in my core.

I may not know much, but I know I am strong
In Lord Jesus, & my grateful heart's full of song,
For when you have Jesus, you've all that you need,
To get through each day, for He loves, guides & feeds.

So, I can't reply when you ask me the time,
But I know I love Christ, I am His & He's mine,
And once I'm in Heaven, I know I'll be cured
Of all earthly ailments, when I'm with my Lord.

The tie between God & I will never break,
No matter when Dementia nags, rattles & aches,
For Salvation's tether is stronger than chain,
Unaffected by illness, grief, heartbreak or pain.

So, thank-you dear Lord, that you don't ever leave,
You stay with your children, their worries relieve,
Dementia may sting like a head full of nettles,
But the joy of The Lord's always there, strong & settled.

BAGGAGE *

As I'm standing on the platform, just about to board the train,
I can't seem to pick my bag up, which is driving me insane!
It's like it's welded to the floor and made of block concrete,
'though I heave and sweat and strain, it still won't budge from by my feet!

I just don't understand it, it's not felt this way before,
So I ask the nearby guard if he could lift it through the door;
"I'm sorry Sir", the guard explains, "You'll have to leave it here",
"But what about my clothes?" I said, "My smokes and cash and beer?"

"Sir, you're not allowed these things upon this Holy train,
They're not needed where you're going and they're of no comfort or gain,
For this train is The Lord's train, Sir, and Heaven the destination,
If you really want to ride it, please leave all baggage at the station!

Your suitcase is too heavy, for it's weighed-down with great sin,
Possessions, pain, resentment, that through the years you have stuffed in!
But there's no place for these things, Sir, aboard this Holy ride,
Just those whose souls have been redeemed are allowed to go inside."

Then a man stops to ask me, offers kindly if I'd like Him to take
The burden of my bag away as HE can lift its heavy weight!
He says that only He can take the sinful contents and my view,
And make me fit for Heaven, as He will restore, revive, renew.

"My friend", He says, "I am The Christ – the one who owns this train,
And all who travel on it I have freed from sin and pain,
You're most welcome to join them, but before the train departs,
You must repent, profess your faith, hold my Spirit in your heart."

Artwork for the poem
"Baggage".

BECAUSE OF THE LIGHT

We can put up with the pouring rain,
And tolerate all kinds of pain,
Repeatedly fend-off The Devil,
And fight bad thoughts that mess and meddle,
Because we know the light is coming.

We can battle-on within the dark,
Press-down anxiety's yelping bark,
Swim through depression's sticky black,
And bear the burdens on our backs,
Because we know the light is coming.

We can manage any type of trial,
Still stand strong at our hundredth mile,
We'll work through every kind of grief,
And shun the Hell that flames beneath,
Because we know the light is coming.

We can weather every sort of ill,
For souls are strong and joyous still,
We'll cope with varied types of angst,
And still know we are blessed – give thanks,
Because we know the light is coming.

We can endure such sorrowed pain,
Fall down on knees, but rise again,
Know we'll be rescued from the dark,
By this light's powerful, divine spark.

The light emits a radiant glow,
Brings hope that God's own children know,
The light is sent from Heaven above,
By our loving Lord, in Grace and love.

The light it soothes and reassures,

Sends comfort, succour and care outpoured,
The light illuminates our path,
Instructs the black to move on past.

The light is fuelled by God himself,
It warms our hearts and makes fear melt,
The light encourages, assures,
That we're protected by The Lord.

The light provides our future's hope,
Which then, in turn, helps us to cope,
The light tells us "Don't be afraid",
Of Satan, sin, death and the grave.

The light is blinding, awesome, Holy,
Touches equally the grand and lowly,
The light brings all to reverent knees,
And draws our prayers and heartfelt pleas.

The light shows us we're not alone,
For there's a God on Heaven's throne,
The light will never fade or dim,
Because this Holy light, is HIM.

POST-CANCER'S STORMY SEAS

I've been eddied, tossed and broken, by this cancer's gripping tide,
Now I'm drifting all alone at sea and don't know how to feel inside,
I see the shore so far away, behind me, where my old-self stands,
What lies ahead is drifting currents, endless skies and shifting sands.

I don't know who I am now, but what I do know is I've changed,
Cancer's altered my whole world and with its eyes my view is rearranged;
I need to find my new self, can't return to yester shores,
But I'm lost, confused, unsettled, still in pain and tired, unsure.

I feel I'm treading water and am frightened I'll just sink,
Now I'm cured I should be happy, but my frazzled brain can't seem to think;
I'm panicked and impatient, apprehensive and don't know,
I'm keen to find a safe new shore but can't see where to go.

When I started this whole journey and was waiting there on cancer's shore,
I pictured the view opposite, where I was healthy, cured, happy once more,
The treatment was the bridge which I would use to cross the storm,
But I fell in troubled waters, which I'm powerless to calm or warm.

I fought the war on cancer, but my battle's still not won,
It's strangled my emotions and its lingering grip is strong,
I thought by now I would be free, unbound from cancer's tether,
But find I'm firmly cast adrift and lacking any clement weather.

But God speaks softly to me, reassures me that He'll help,
He knows the trial I'm going through and hears each struggled, woeful yelp,
He understands my circumstance and says He's got it all in hand,
That I need to exercise my faith and in due course I will reach dry land.

The Lord's my rubber-ring and raft, my lifeboat and supporter,
And He knows the plans He has for me, as His beloved daughter,
For now I must swim patiently, across this new and challenging sea,
And trust that God will lead me on, to the person I'm supposed to be.

For God will keep my head above the surface and won't let me drown,
And He'll strengthen my muscles, so the numbness cannot drag me down,
The Lord will build my stamina, make me wiser, give me cause to fight,
And then I'll be renewed, refreshed, ever-grateful for His grace and might.

THE LIGHT AT THE END OF THE TUNNEL *

I'm groping along all these darkened stone walls,
Which seem to have no end or corners at all,
They're arching around me on every side,
And over the top, which entraps me inside.

The bricks are so harsh and are all ashened black,
And mould and decay lies in all of the cracks,
These walls are just dripping with poisonous sludge,
'though I rub and I wipe, still the grime will not budge.

In this tunnel the bricks are unyielding and dense,
It's so quiet down here, which makes it intense,
The floor is quite slippery, dirty and damp,
Every footstep I take makes my legs shake and cramp.

Down here in the dark I hear sewer rats squeak,
And the air and the atmosphere's so cold and bleak,
I'm calling for aid and I pace, scream and shout,
But there's nobody coming to help me get out.

Some of the brickwork is jagged, digs in,
Which leaves cuts and scratches and wounds on my skin,
They sting and they hurt and are bound to leave scars,
On the inside and out I've been left bruised and marred.

This cold, dark, dank tunnel is built of my life,
Bad memories past and all present-day strife,
Transgressions and errors, woes, struggles, regrets,
Abuse and self-loathing, rejection, neglect.

Things that I didn't do, things that I did,
And some things so shameful they need to stay hid,
The dark of frustration refuses to fade,
Or yield to the promise of happier days.

These menacing walls begin whispering, creaking,
Closing in on me now as they're moving and creeping,
Escaping the past is a challenging fight,
When it plays on my mind and has teeth that still bite.

I cannot dwell happily down in this dark,
Where noises can startle, and the future is stark,
What's down here to motivate, bring me some hope?
Reassure and uphold me, and help me to cope?

As I'm gazing along these unwelcoming walls,
A soft light appears, looks inviting, yet small,
A thin tiny chink that the darkness resists,
Still it doggedly grows and so strongly persists.

It beckons me onwards, away from the black,
It fills me with hope and says not to look back,
I follow this light full of promise and love,
And know that it's pure, sent from Heaven above.

The nearer I get, so much brighter the glow,
It is like morning sunshine on icy fresh snow,
The closer I stumble, the less that I see,
Of the cold, dark surroundings that try to haunt me.

The more focused I am, the more intense the light,
'til I'm shielding my eyes, just to preserve my sight!
My head becomes lowered, knees drop to the floor,
When God's love surrounds, I lay prostrate in awe.

Whilst I know that behind me the darkness still lurks,
And there's stuff from my past that will still and hurt,
I reborn, renewed, so now don't seem to care,
Because I've seen the light, and the power that's there.

**Artwork for the poem
"The Light At The End Of The Tunnel".**

BOUNCER

"I'm sorry, but you can't come in",
The bouncer tells the guy,
Who's furious and questions,
Other people who get by.

For some of them are paupers,
With no prospects or careers,
There are criminals and outcasts,
Those looked-down on by their peers.

There're people from all nations,
Backgrounds, gender, age and race,
But each one walks with confidence,
Knowing they'll get in through Grace.

The man argues he's "better",
Than these others going through,
Who haven't got a posh car,
Lots of cash, designer shoes.

He says he has a good job,
Owns a business, is 'the boss',
But the bouncer still won't budge,
And now the man is at a loss.

He persists, winks at the bouncer,
Hands him money on the side,
But the big man just refuses,
Says he can't and won't take bribes!

The man then tries persuasion,
Flattery and threats and more,
He throws a punch and makes a scene,
But is still barred from the door!

"Don't you know just who I am?"
The man proceeds to shout,
"Indeed I do", comes the reply,
"Which is why you're staying out!"

"I have a list", the bouncer says,
"And if your name's not on,
I've been informed to ban you;
To let you in would just be wrong!"

The man then asks what he must do,
To get his name on there,
Complains that it's 'his right',
'What he deserves' and it's 'not fair!'

The bouncer sternly looks at him,
And speaks in a firm voice,
Explains it's all his own fault,
For in his life he had a choice –

The man had many chances
To have his name put on the list,
But thought that he knew better,
And due to ego, did resist.

The way to enter in
Is through Christ Jesus, God The Son,
Regardless who you are,
Or what you have or haven't done.

You won't get in through bribery,
Nor tears or charm or rage,
For your name needs to be written,
On the Book of Life's blessed page.

Now it's too late to change his mind,
So the man's been turned away,
Must go towards the other place,

Where there'll be Hell to pay.

He's filled with shame and sorrow,
Lamentations and regrets,
Hangs his sad head in acceptance,
And slowly walks back down the steps.

BATTLE SCARS

Everyone has battle scars,
Whether they're outside or in,
They could be from a mental fight,
Which won't show on the skin.

Maybe you're still battling-on?
And not yet left with scars?
For now, the wound is gaping, fresh,
And healing seems so far.

You might have many ancient scars,
From traumas in the past,
Which you now accept and can move on,
Be reconciled at last.

You could be in the process,
Of accepting your own mark?
Which may be seen upon your skin
Or buried within your head and heart.

Whatever type of scars you have,
The Lord does not reject,
And loves each single marking,
That WE have issues to accept.

But try to challenge all your scars,
With a fresh and different view,
See them as a badge of honour,
For all that you've been through.

For you fought so well in battle,
Stand victorious, still alive,
And in God's loving, Gracious care,
You'll continue to survive.

POINTLESS (Satan's halo) *

Satan is scheming alone in the dark,
The only light down here's from one of two sparks,
The first orange glow is from Hell fire itself,
The second, from something he's trying to melt.
For Satan is hammering, shaping and melding,
Using tools and an anvil, he's sweating and welding,
Attempting to remake the thing that he lost,
When God took it from him at a terrible cost.

For Satan is trying to make a new halo,
From worthless earth metal and brimstone below,
He misses its status, for it made him feel proud,
Gave a sense of importance to stand out from the crowd.
Satan yearns for a head-piece that's equal in measure,
To an angelic halo - a most divine treasure,
He wants something shiny for others to see,
To inspire their worship and prompt bended knee.

For that's Satan's problem and was all along,
He was never content to give God praise and song,
He wanted the power and glory alone,
And so set to conspire to take The Lord's throne.
Then a battle ensued between angels and demons,
The Lord and the Devil, and it stands to reason,
That of course The Lord won, for He rules over all,
And as punishment Satan and his demons did fall.

They were stripped of their title, privileges and power,
And thrown from the top of their ivory tower,
Their robes and their halos were also removed,
Which was to be expected, and none were bemused.
Satan and his followers were duly cast-out,
And banished from Heaven by The Lord's Holy clout,
There was screaming and wailing and gnashing of teeth,
When they fell down from Glory to Hades beneath.

How foolish of Satan to think he'll replace,
A halo that's Holy and gifted in Grace,
It's made of God's promises and Holy light,
Can't be re-created by greed in the night.
So Satan will try 'til the world comes to cease,
To make his own halo, but he can't make this piece,
And from now 'til destruction he'll labour in vain,
Be frustrated that he'll never have victor's gain.

Artwork for the poem
"Pointless" (Satan's halo).

THE FORTRESS INSIDE ME

I know an awesome fortress, which has stood for quite some time,
The outer stone is mossy, covered in a layer of dirty slime,
It doesn't look that fancy, but will shelter me through Winter storms,
Cruel winds may come to buffet, but within the walls, it's calm and warm.

This fortress was held under siege, by cancer and depression,
Which tried to break the stonework, but it grew, defying this oppression,
Slabs are looking tired and marked, the corners chipped and tattered,
But structurally it's sturdy, despite all the trials that leave it battered.

Satan shoots his flaming arrows high and low to weaken walls,
And strikes at the foundation, using tricks and lies and demon hoards,
This fortress will not crumble, for is built upon the cornerstone,
Its faith remains unshakable, since The Holy Spirit set up home.

Within this divine fortress, living happily is my saved soul,
Resting safe, within God's care, where once there was a gaping hole,
But faith and trust and Holy love have filled that void with fortressed rock,
Which keeps my soul protected, against trials, attacks, all storms and shocks.

There's nothing that can breach these walls, they'll not erode and never fall,
But keep on building every day, in saving grace, they're strong and tall,
This fortress built within me's held together by The Victor's blood,
So stands firmly unshaken, throughout fire and pain and raging floods.

The bricks are laid by God Himself and cannot fade or come undone,
'though my sin takes their shine off, they are gleaming within Christ, The Son,
And, one day my faith's fortress will be finished, to the Lord's delight,
Then I will dwell, forever, in His heavens and see joy's pure light.

AN EVERYDAY PILGRIM

As an every-day pilgrim, I come to the cross,
Reflect on Christ's glory, His suffering and loss,
As I gratefully pray, I look to Jesus' face,
And thank Him, in reverence, for taking my place.

Sometimes I can come to Him striding along,
Relaxed in contentment, with heart full of song,
Kiss the cross where its base stands firmly in the ground,
Marvel at all it means to this joy that I've found.

But, most times I struggle, I won't tell a lie,
Fighting everyday battles to just get on by,
I'm physically weary and often in pain,
And with each tired step, just an inch I can gain.

Mental hardships are worst, make me fuzzy and lag,
'though I try to walk tall my hurt head makes me sag;
Some days it's an effort to rise and get dressed,
But I know in Christ Jesus I'm still saved and blessed.

So I make my trip daily to get to the cross,
'though depression's dark drags and anxieties toss,
It might take all day, but I'll crawl if I have-to,
For God is my love and the one my soul clings-to.

The road to the cross is full of distractions,
To steer us away and pull at sin's reactions,
The world does encourage us just to be selfish,
Leading us from God as the heart's only wish.

For we're weak in our flesh and so easily swayed,
It doesn't take much to lure us and persuade,
We think we know better and can manage fine,
That we don't need our God and we haven't the time!

The Devil himself is waiting by the road,
That leads to the cross, just to increase our load,
He makes us feel guilty 'bout the sins we carry,
Says God will reject us, tries to make us tarry.

He grabs at our ankles and claws at our minds,
To get us to leave Christ and the cross behind,
The Devil will bite us and whisper such lies,
He'll make sure we trip-up, will scratch out our eyes.

But I'll still persevere with my pilgrimage daily,
'though I'm crawling along, and my eyes can't see clearly,
For I know that my faith brings me to the cross,
And it won't let me falter, even when I'm lost.

For God gifts me strength which does draw me along,
'though I'm struggling, my soul remains full of song,
So, it really won't matter if other things grasp,
I'll still touch the cross daily, 'til my final gasp.

And on my last day upon this mortal coil,
'though I can't kiss the cross, The Devil is still foiled,
For Jesus Himself, from His Heavenly throne,
Will send down an angel to carry me home.

And when I'm in Glory, all struggles will cease,
As I'll dwell with Lord Jesus, forever, in peace,
All hurt will be healed and pains will go away,
But 'til then, I'm a grateful pilgrim . . . every day.

HOPE IN THE DARKEST OF PLACES *

Jet-black is the colour of the straight-jacket I wear,
It's the colour of my frightened tears, the sweat that's in my hair.
Jet-black is the colour of the brick wall in my head,
And the sticky, inky, oozing tide that fills my brain with dread.

Jet-black is the colour of the snake that's wrapped-around
My neck and arms and ribcage and squeezes whilst I'm bound.
Jet-black is the colour of the ceiling, floor and walls,
Of this padded-cell I'm trapped in, where I feel helpless and small.

Jet-black is the colour of the smog that's in the air,
It's the deathly hopeless silence when I scream but no-one's there.
Jet-black is the colour of the ash that's on the floor,
And depression's keys that jangle in the padlock on the door.

But then I see a spider gently crawl across the room,
And it's back is brightly shining which illuminates the gloom,
My eyes are fixed upon it in a captivating gaze,
'though it's small I sense it's mighty, so my hopes are quickly raised.

This tiny, light arachnid potters over to the wall,
And in the corner of my cell spins out a thread so small,
But quickly it transforms into a shining mighty web,
Which slowly draws the blackness out from my depressive head.

The snake that's wrapped around me cannot stand this blinding light,
It uncoils, and then shrinks away from the power, shining bright,
For The Lord has made this spider and has sent her to my aid,
Her web overrules the padded-cell that depression's dark has made.

She unpicks all the buckles on my jacket so I'm freed,
And tends and binds the deep cuts that my mental ills made bleed,
She reassures and calms me as she sits upon my hand,
And reminds me to have patience in whatever God has planned.

I see an image of the cross upon her glowing back,
Which warms my heart for Jesus and brings comfort in this black,
The web increases in size and the Holy light gets brighter,
It gives the room a cosy glow and my mental ills feel lighter.

Now I can breathe, feel more relaxed, and contemplate this trial,
Try to see the lessons I can learn and rest with God a while.
I know despite how dark it gets, God's light will still reach me,
And however small it may appear, it's all the chink I need.

**Artwork for the poem
"Hope In The Darkest Of Places".**

SANCTUARY

Only God holds the key to this room,
The room where I'm loved and I'm free,
The place where I'm always accepted,
And never once struggle to breathe.

This room is private and built just for me,
It's the place where I can scream and shout,
And fall on my knees to confess to The Lord
All the things that I'm upset about.

In this room nobody can see me,
Here no-one will tell me a lie,
I am free to vent my frustrations,
For The Lord hears all things that I cry.

I can show God my vulnerability,
And admit when I'm scared and afraid,
Unobserved by the world I can confess,
And repent all the mistakes I've made.

In this room I can be alone with God,
No-holds-barred, I can fly and be free!
I can drop the brave-face that I wear every day,
The mask everybody else sees.

Only God holds the key to this room
But He's no jailer, He keeps me protected,
For He built this room as my sanctuary,
And a place where I'm never rejected.

NOTHING CAN OUTSHINE THE LORD

Enchanting droplets in fields of dew,
The blinding rays of the sun at noon,
Twinkling stars in the black velvet night,
The piercing streams of silvery moonlight.
Dancing glimmers on ocean waves,
Dragonflies glinting, on summer days,
Metalic shine of the humming-bird's plume,
A chandelier's sparkle that lights up the room.
Nuggets of gold ore found in miner's pans,
The cut-diamond ring on a fiance's hand,
The excitement of Christmas in small children's eyes,
Encrusted jewels on the white dress of a bride.
Glaring reflections off squeaky-clean glass,
Polished shells of green beetles as they scuttle past,
The glittering patterns of butterfly wings,
The shimmering scales of each fish as it swims.
Vibrant petals on beautiful flowers,
The glittering frost, during Winter's dark hours,
The mirrored, buffed shine on a fine leather shoe,
The sky seen at dusk, with its scarlet, pink hue . . . .

Not one of these things can begin to compare
To the glory of God and the Holy light there,
The Lamb's spotless coat glistens, pure as fresh snow,
And His victory and grace give a luminous glow.
God's love through The Christ shines throughout all the earth,
And no mountains of gold measure up to the worth
Of Redemption, Salvation, via Jesus, The Son,
Through faith in the cross and His great Resurrection.

Now reigning in glory, wearing robe and a sash,
Christ's eyes blaze like fire, brighter than lightning flash,
His feet glowing bronze, as if made in a furnace,
His voice sounds like water, which does rush and chase.
He holds seven stars in the palm of His hand,

Hair looks white, like wool, on Jesus, Son of Man,
Coming out of His mouth is a double-edged sword,
Face shines like the sun . . . for such light is The Lord.

And nothing on earth can outshine or compete
With the joy our souls feel, as we fall at His feet,
For happy souls glow in contentment and peace,
When we receive our crown and live eternal bliss.

CAGED *

Just a small ugly chick in a hard metal cage,
That mental ills, traumas and stresses have made,
I feel so restricted and long to fly free,
But my wings are too broken and will not support me.

So I'm hopping around and scratching at the base,
Of my cage, as the tears gently fall down my face,
I'm feeling so helpless and hopeless and small,
For I can't reach the hatch, as the cage is too tall.

My fears and self-doubt keep on swelling and growing,
These steel bars get thicker without me even knowing,
Satan likes to come along and rattle my cage,
Tells me that no-one loves me and laughs as I fade.

But just when I think I may shrivel and die,
The Lord sends me prompting and gives strength inside,
Emboldens me to glare-at and stare-out the Devil,
Motivates me to defy the toughened cage metal.

I know God could just come and rip off the top,
Of this harsh, problematic and cold metal box,
But He says that He won't, for the time is not right,
As I need to grow stronger, before taking flight.

So, I patiently wait, and as I bide my time,
God strengthens my body, my soul and my mind,
He nurtures and feeds me and tends to my wounds,
And ensures that I receive all Spiritual foods.

Now my legs are much stronger, I can get them running,
And I sense that the time very soon may be coming,
When I will break free from this tiresome small cage,
And freely fly-off, to begin a new age!

For I'm no more a helpless and hopeless small chick,
But a fine mighty eagle, whose talons are thick,
And my wings are now long and won't fit inside
The confines of this cage, for they're too big and wide.

So, I flex and prepare them and stretch through the bars,
Fix my eyes on the Heavens, reach my mind to the stars,
Keep my heart and soul focused on The Lord up above,
Knowing that I'm held safe in his mercy and love.

I'm excited to think about all the new steps,
That The Lord has planned for me, and whatever is next,
My trust in His wisdom, allows me to cope,
So I'll wait on His timing, and relax in His hope.

Artwork for the poem
"Caged".

MOVING HOUSE

I'm excited but also nervous, as I'm moving house today,
I shall miss my friends and neighbours, for I'm going far away,
I feel a pang as I look back, at the home I've known for years,
It holds memories both good and bad, which makes me shed a tear.

I think about my brand new home, the one I'm moving into,
Don't know how long the journey is, or how I'll feel at being new,
I'm hoping I'll fit in okay, not sure what everyone expects,
I feel a little trepidation, but am happy for what's coming next.

This house move is a strange one, like no other move I've made before,
For I haven't packed a single thing, nor got a key for the front door,
I'm taking nothing with me, for I won't need my belongings,
For everything I'll ever want is already waiting at my lodgings.

And I know the main guy in charge, He's such a kind and lovely man,
He's always been a good friend and through struggles always holds my hand,
He's sent a guide to help me move, from this dwelling to the next,
But it isn't a removals firm and there is no van as you'd expect.

Because the place I'm moving to, is a room within my Father's house,
And Heaven's the Holy destination of this new abode I talk about,
The man in charge is Jesus Christ, my best friend, Lord and Saviour,
In whom I'm granted access, and not through MY merit or behaviour.

An angel is my moving guy, to help show me to Glory,
To drop me off at Heaven's gate, to begin my new eternal story,
And Christ Himself will welcome me, for knows my faith is proven strong,
Clothed in HIS great righteousness, to serve in Heaven's where I belong.

I don't know what the journey's like, from this world to the next,
But I trust entirely in my Lord, so I won't waste time in getting stressed,
I've trusted my God throughout life, and I'll trust Him much more in my death,
And Christ said He'll be waiting, to see me face to face, when I've no more breath.

It matters not what like Heaven's like, the finer details large or small,
The journey, or the dwelling place, for Christ will oversee it all,
As long I am with The Lord, as he promised, that's where my heart lies,
And my soul will be happy, dwelling in God's house, in Heaven's skies.

BROKEN POTTERY

Life's troubles often chip away
At the surface of this painted clay,
Leave the pottery appearing tattered,
Cracked in places and somewhat battered.
Stresses heat can leave it charred,
Depression breaks it into shards,
Whilst pain and grief cause it to pile
In shattered fragments, for a while.

But then The Lord, who first made man,
Scoops up the remnants in His hands,
And puts the pieces back together,
Fixed with love, in grace, forever.
And 'though it's so hard when we break,
God will a new creation make,
From dusty slivers on the floor,
He remoulds us into so much more.

I'M NOT A SUN WORSHIPPER, BUT I AM A SON WORSHIPPER! *

I don't really like the bright summer sun!
It's merciless in showing-up all my flaws,
The myriad of imperfections on my pasty white face.
It makes me sweat with its scorching heat,
And its mighty rays burn my delicate skin.
I long for some relief from its harshness.
I need soothing shade
From the sun's torturing glare.

But there is one who's light I DO want
To burn brightly on me!
Not the sun, but The SON –
God-The-Son, Christ Jesus.
He sees my flaws and loves me still.
He knows my many imperfections -
The ones on the inside that no-one else sees,
And He loves me still.
The Son's light burns brighter than the ordinary sun!
His rays won't burn out, nor burn my skin
For I am protected by faith.
I am forgiven.
I will not sweat in the glare of God's power,
For I am confident in Jesus' promise and sacrifice.
I cannot hide from Christ's light,
Nor do I wish to.
His light is love, Grace, mercy, soothing,
And reassuring like nothing else!
I will happily, gratefully, humbly, stand in Jesus's light,
Forever and ever.
For THIS Son is good!

Artwork for the poem
"I'm Not A Sun Worshipper, But I Am A Son Worshipper!"

NAKED BEFORE GOD

I'm naked before God above,
For He knows all my hidden parts,
He sees the secret tears at night,
And feels the sorrows of my heart,
I'm naked, as I cannot hide,
Nor camouflage the way I feel,
Before our ever-knowing Lord -
A Holy bond is open . . . real.

And so the sin I hold inside,
Is open for our God to see,
Exposed, my broken soul laid bare
Is filthy, dirty as can be,
But Jesus takes me as I am,
In truth and faith and trust,
The Spirit comes to cleanse within -
My joyous heart is fit to bust!

But I still feel quite guilty,
And I shudder now, as am afraid,
For I'm in line at Heaven's gate,
And stand unworthy, bowed, ashamed,
But my name's in The Book of Life,
So promptly I am ushered through,
'though still I'm feeling nervous,
As the throne of God comes into view.

For I'm naked and embarrassed,
Can't defend my right to Heaven's place
That's possible through Jesus,
Faith and love and The Lord's saving Grace.
My heart pounds and my legs give way,
I kneel before God's judgement throne,
No mortal kin to help me out
As I give life's account . . . alone.

But, then, someone comes to the fore,
As I quake in my lack of dress,
Lord Jesus comes to stand by me -
Gift me HIS robes of Righteousness.
With power and love He covers me,
So I am blemish free and brave,
For Christ The Lord has redeemed me -
I'm freed from sin and hellish grave.

With Jesus I need fear no wrath,
As stand in Him on judgement day,
For His blood makes me spotless white,
His victory takes my sin away.
And He clothes me in royal robes,
I know I don't deserve or earn,
Without them, I'd be sent to Hell,
Where teeth do gnash and souls do burn.

So, thank you Jesus that you came
And that Salvation comes through you,
That every vow is faithful,
And that every word you say is true,
That you accept our nakedness,
And see our sin, but want us still,
And love us all so much in Grace,
That you went up to Calvary's hill.

THIEF

I don't consider myself a fraud or a thief,
But somehow feel that's what I am!
For I'm taking everything that my soul needs,
From the mouth of this crucified man,
With every shudder of agony He takes,
And with each shallow breath that He's breathing,
I feel myself going from death into life
And my own pain and sorrow relieving.

I'm inhaling His goodness and righteousness,
Absorbing His lack of iniquity,
The harder He nails all sin to the cross,
The more I can feel the curse setting me free.
And in His final minutes of mortal life,
When He takes a last look round the earth,
His work is completed, and I can be cleansed
By HIS blood that pours down on the dirt.

Then on the third day when He's risen to life,
I too hitch a ride from the grave,
For only Christ Jesus, as God, conquers death,
But I gain from the victories HE made.
And then I can walk into His home,
Take off my own clothes, dirty and black,
Exchange them for HIS robes of Glory –
Spotless white with fine wings on the back.

I remove my thief's dark balaclava,
And smooth all my ruffled hair down,
Go into HIS great hall in the cupboard,
Grasp life's prize and then put on the crown.
I know I feel like an imposter –
There's no way I deserve to be here,
I'm embarrassed when Jesus approaches,
And can't look in His eyes when He's near.

But, Christ's loving hand reaches to me,
He says I am no robber or thief,
For what I have taken is God's GIFT,
When I showed Him faith, trust and belief.
And you can't steal something that's given,
He explains with a smile on His face,
He agrees that I do not deserve this,
But tells me that's the whole point of GRACE!

God's happy for mankind to share in The Son,
And indeed that is why He first came,
For there's no way to steal our Salvation –
It is gifted when we trust in His name.
The Lord knows that we're sinful, weak, selfish,
And sees the great foibles of Man,
But He loves us and wants us regardless,
And can save us via The Spotless Lamb.

ABLAZE

Now, please don't be mistaken,
When you view my life as ash,
See the smouldering remains of joy,
And tears on each burnt eyelash,
My feet are charred and weary,
And my eyes sting with the smoke,
The clouds and debris in the air,
Cause me to gasp and choke.

For stresses, strains and traumas,
Mental pain, physical ails,
Have burned away my happiness,
And left my peace to flail,
There are merely only fragments,
Of positivity now left,
So you may look, be thinking,
That my faith in God's bereft.

But you're very much mistaken,
As the blaze that you can see,
Burning brightly in the centre,
Isn't Hell fire as it seems,
But purifying flames from God,
And my soul's strength and spark,
Burning with love and passion,
For The Lord, amidst the dark.

For all the troubles on this earth,
Can't quench these fearsome flames,
Which warm, support and comfort,
Throughout all life's trials and pains.
And my heart burns forever,
For my God, my love, my Lord,
And if you listen carefully,
You'll hear the flames do roar!

The Holy Spirit stokes this fire,
And keeps it all ablaze,
So it can never peter-out,
Not even on dark days,
For during times of trouble,
Is when this fire burns its brightest,
And when my heart is heaviest,
Is when my soul is lightest.

For God's Grace is its strongest,
When I'm struggling and weak,
And The Spirit that dwells in me,
Roars with power when I can't speak.
Look closer still at The Lord's fire -
You'll see me in the centre,
Just strolling around with Jesus Christ,
All-powerful sustainer and creator.

And He'll ensure I am not scorched,
By fire or tribulations,
And I will rise to sing his praise,
To every doubting nation,
For God sends me all trying times,
To then build me afresh,
So I fly like a phoenix,
And The Lord's my solid nest!

HANGING BY A THREAD *

The rope that I once held secure,
Has now worn thin and feels unsure,
I find I'm hanging by a thread,
And feel consumed with fear and dread.
For as I dangle off life's shelf,
I find it hard to stop myself,
From slowly spinning round and round,
I fret I'll fall & hit the ground.

My sweaty fingers start to slip,
I struggle now to keep my grip,
I'm getting in a panicked state,
Thinking this thread can't hold my weight.
For my rope just weathered and frayed,
Through hardship, pain and stormy days,
And all that's left is this one strand,
Which I wind tight around my hand.

But then God comes to reassure,
Says he will keep it strong, secure,
Won't let the last thread snap and break,
To plummet me and my life take.
He's confident that I'll hold tight,
Grip to this thread with all my might,
But says that if I WERE to fall,
He'd catch me before I could call!

For God is always there for me,
My safety net, spread out securely,
Sturdy hands forever braced,
To help me in His loving Grace.
And there's no time He won't be there,
I'm safe in His great Holy care,
So I relax, no longer dread,
Despite I still hang by a thread.

Artwork for the poem
"Hanging By A Thread".

PLAYGROUND

(A collaboration between Michael Grgich and Suzanne Newman)

Woke-up before the sunrise, I'm still drenched and covered in the dark,
Trying to find strength to face the day, with a hollow soul, and empty heart,
Finding two feet beneath me and those feet are ready to make a start,
So I follow them as they carry me, down the street, towards my local park.

Through teary eyes I wonder . . . my stumbling steps not even seen,
Running from the emptiness, running frantic from emotional debris.
Every puppet on Earth posts their sin - that shame cannot be veiled,
Every string from Heaven then was cut, to give to us this mortal world.
But we dismissed . . . voided the call . . . shutdown ears and we turned away,
So as a whole - a kin, a species, we missed what The Lord had to say.

So, looking to the playground, and then gazing from upon the swing,
I am an adult, still a child in Christ, I sit down and kick up my feet,
I embrace the swing . . . the wind caressing me.

And, as I sit here, gently swinging, moving to and fro,
I ponder at this thing called "life" - its tides and trials that ebb and flow.
I look towards the see-saw, which, as real life, rides us up and down,
The round-a-bout, spins us in circles, going no-where but just round and round.
The climbing-frame looks daunting, as we stand at the bottom, looking up,
But gives different perspective, when we've scaled its heights and reached the top.

I wonder why God made us? Why . . . .when all along He knew we'd fall,
Give in to base temptations, feel the lure and pull of selfish calls.
I ponder what's the point of life? What lessons are there we must learn?
In order to be fit for Heaven, and not dwell where hellfire burns.

So, sitting in the sand and tan bark, looking up towards the skies,
I thank God for His guidance and for teaching us how to ride these rides.
Looking to the grassy field, I see so much new, innocent life,

Children kicking about the soccer balls, no sign of sin within their eyes.
It teaches me humility, it teaches me to strive for so much more,
It teaches to me, my life is not forgotten, and we were all sinless when we were born.
On the playground it becomes so clear . . . what a life and soul are for,
On the playground Christ's children are free to frolic and play,
For His children bear no thorns.
The sun warms me as I watch them,
And as I watch, the true SON warms my soul,
I don't ever want to leave this park,
Never want to let this feeling go.

I ponder why and when as adults, we turn to sin so readily?
Think we know better than the Lord – who creates and sustains everything!
Life used to be so simple . . . purer motivations . . . much more love,
No scepticism as kids . . . less greed . . . easier to be near God above.

I push much harder on the ground, and use my feet to move the swing,
I soar as far as I can reach, and wish I could touch Christ, The King,
But I am nowhere near the perfect skies of Heaven and its peace,
Trapped in the dirt of this world's hurt, where struggles and pain never cease.
One day I'll be in God's playground - in Glory where there's endless bliss,
His precious child . . . reborn . . . perfected, no more tears . . . nothing amiss,
Innocent and pure once more, like the children I see playing there,
In the field, right by this playground, with their laughing eyes and carefree air.

I thank the Lord for gifting hope, for Salvation through God The Son -
The only way that sinful chains and Satan's grasp can be undone.
So I will do my best in life, and be encouraged everyday
In this earthly playground we call life, which rides us hard in many ways.
For throughout all the ups and downs, and each time we fall and get hurt,
God's there to help and guide us, pick us up and dust off all the dirt.
Without Lord Jesus, we would find we'd just stay helpless, spinning round,
But in Him we have focus, and the promise of our Heaven's crown.

Written jointly by Michael Grgich (MAG) & Suzanne Newman.

KINDRED SPIRITS – PART TWO

ALL POEMS WRITTEN BY
MICHAEL GRGICH (MAG)

ARTWORK BY DEBRA WHELAN

(All rights reserved)

CONTENTS – (* = ACCOMPANIED BY ARTWORK)

1 - WELCOME TO MY MIND
2 - HEATHEN TO HEAVEN *
3 – QUICKSAND
4 - TWO EQUALS ONE
5 – DEPTHS *
6 - SATAN'S THRONE
7 – BROKEN WINGS
8 – CHAIN OF LIFE *
9 - GOD'S PINOCCHIO
10 – LOST
11 - THE CROSS
12 - THE BATTLE FOR ETERNITY
13 – CRACKED
14 – PRAY TM *
15 – THE AFTERNOW
16 – PARADISE
17 – THE DARK *
18 – FREIGHT TRAIN
19 - IN THE MIRROR
20 - BLESSINGS *
21 - THE STORM
22 - BROKEN ROAD
23 – WINGS
24 – WATERFALL *
25 – THE VOICE
26 – DIG
27 – RELEASE *
28 – SEVEN NAILS
29 - A TIRED OLD MAN
30 – THE CALL
31 – YOU HEAL ME *
32 - MY DAY OF JUDGEMENT

WELCOME TO MY MIND

Welcome WORLD to my mind, please follow me inside,
Don't be frightened, do not hide, just stay close tight by my side.

Emotions become nature, that's fact in the inner me,
So look around and I'll explain the Emotions you will see,

LET'S PROCEED! . . . YOU WITH ME? . . .

The thunder-storm in the distance, drenching rain upon the plains,
That is worldly stress and pressure, Earthly wounds and pain,

The mighty oak majestic, thick, anchored deep into the ground,
That is my foundation, where my will and strength are found,

The sunlight that we bask in, and its warmth, are my family,
Reminding me of the guidance and love they each offer unto me.

The forest thicket greenery, are my feelings for all of man,
Hoping someday, maybe, every one of us in unity will stand,

They're put away right now, but if I allowed out all my rage,
You'd be swallowed up in firestorms, tornadoes and earthquakes,

See that endless vast deep blue sea? That's love flowing free from me,
For every creature, every being, every plant and every tree,

Finally, take a deep breath in, feel the air in your whole as you breathe,
That's Love, belief, and Faith in Christ who gave all of this to you and me,

Without the air, without the breath, the rest of my mind would die,
Jesus pumps love into my soul and breathes life into my mind.

Well, I guess the tour is over now, time to step back outside my mind,
Thank you for the visit . . . Y'all comeback now, anytime!

HEATHEN TO HEAVEN *

Born to a Catholic home, where for all sin you must atone,
Raised strict but raised with love. All praise be to above!
In adolescence the wicked courted me, offered amazing, tempting dreams,
So, an innocent soul fell astray, from Jesus Christ I ran away!

I FELL . . .

Debauchery and sin, I let that world in!
Hell, let it in? I embraced it, I wanted every day to taste it!
No one mattered only ME! . . . I WAS A GOD, CAN NO-ONE SEE?
I HURT THE PEOPLE DEAR TO ME, JUST TO PROVE THAT GOD WAS ME . . .

I WAS A FOOL . . .

I hit life at warp-speed, drugs, sex, money, and greed,
Living phat and living large, behind the curtain, the Devil in charge!

A tainted soul knighted a Heathen,
However, the story has yet to begin . . .

Decades lost listening to the eerie, cold wicked,
Sinning off the cuff, grinning as I did,

I WAS LOST . . .

Wandering dark highways, trying to find a road,
I was done hurting people, but it's all I'd ever known,
An earthly angel intervened, that day I choose to leave this land,
Introducing me to the only one, who truly, honestly understands . . . .

PRAISE BE TO CHRIST!

Jesus this is Michael, Michael meet Jesus Christ!
An atom bomb within my heart burst not once, but twice!

I knew in a fraction of a heartbeat, this was the path I need,
I knew before I even had a thought, dropped happy to me knees.

I FOUND YOU!

From here I HAD to learn HIM, from here I HAD to love,
A Heathen heart was dying, no longer pumping blood . . .

I WANT YOU JESUS!

Chose to bathe myself in Jesus' love, underwater to cleanse sin,
Dedicate my life to Him, a life just about to begin!

I'M CLEANSING SIN!

Up out of the water, started a life anew,
A washed soul filled with love and grace in Heathen absence grew,
To the Scripture, to the chapel, to my 1 on 1's with Christ,
Each moment I am in His grace seems like an endless night.
When I had my children, after, I could not imagine life without,
I feel the same way now with Christ, I am faithful and devote.
I will never waver, I will die loving Jesus, loving man,
Remaining life devoted to reaching His promised land . . .
It's been a twisty, turny, rollercoaster full speed twenty-four-seven,
But that's the story of the Heathen who fought his way to Heaven!

I AM WHOLE!
I AM SAVED BY ABOVE!
I AM CLEANSED!
BY SAVIOR JESUS' LOVE.
I AM LOVED!

**Artwork for the poem
"Heathen To Heaven".**

QUICKSAND

Looking into the darkness, unafraid to take a stand,
The Devil taunts me daily, begs of me "Boy, take my hand"!

I cast away the serpent, I will NOT follow his demands!
Satan curls and cries, 'tis a Devil in quicksand.

"I will not take your hand"!

Everyday day, his Darkness comes at me, offering treasures and ecstasy,
My eyes 'though, they realize, his lies are not for me,
I can proudly stand, against the dark evil in this land,
Telling the Devil "I'm with Christ, hit the damn quicksand"!

"I will NOT take your hand!" . . .

"I won't believe in YOU, only Jesus Christ is true,
I know just what to do . . . I'll throw my own quicksand at you"!

"Bury in it, Satan!
You can't have me, you're mistaken.

I am a champion for Christ,
Ain't no quicksand for me tonight!
So, struggle aimless Satan, struggle against the light,
YOU'RE drowning in the quicksand, you're in FULL and DEEP tonight!
I'm a soul devoted to Jesus, my soul is already saved,
I won't stray from the Holy light with Jesus Christ I bathe"!

"I'll give you every desire, I will make you whole life grand"!
The Devil tells me smiling, begging of me to take his hand,
Twitching in my forearm fighting extention of my hand,
Whip it back, with violent faith, banishing the Devil to quicksand . . .

"I WILL NEVER TAKE YOUR HAND"!

TWO EQUALS ONE

Dear lord, please hear your son,
By thy will all will be done,
Knee bent to the chosen Son,
Servant to you, armor strapped on.

Because one is none,
But two are one.

I will not leave, I will not run,
Thankful for the peace in soul begun,
I thank you Christ, for what you've done,
Sheltering me from the darkness come.

Because one is none,
And two are one.

I've lived without a thought to none,
Only focused on me, my own run,
A fool, who since has seen The Son,
No longer running from the one.

Because one is none,
And two are one.

Even when the shadows choose to come,
I posted up I did not run,
Screaming the name of The chosen Son,
I held my ground to show WE'RE ONE!

I DEFEATED THE ONE,
SHOWING I BELIEVE THAT TWO ARE ONE.

I didn't cower Lord, I did not run,
I knew that this war could be won,
Even when the darkness comes,

I will soldier, I will not run,
Opening/giving a soul to you, THAT WAS ONCE UNDONE!
REALIZING FINALLY,
THAT ONE IS NONE,
AND WITH YOU, CHRIST, TWO IS ALWAYS ONE.

So whatever arrows shadows shoot at me, I will dodge every one,
Take a knee and pray to thee, The true chosen Son,
And my soul will rejoice in Heaven, when my life on Earth is done,
Because I know that One equals NOTHING!
But with Christ TWO EQUALS ONE! AMEN.

DEPTHS *

The deep is taking me . . .
Lost and abandoned in deep blue sea,
Having trouble seeing what I need,
To float on top, above the deep.

The depths claim the all of me . . .
Tied to blind eyes, so I can't see,
I try to rub them, to clear debris,
But the deep depths have stolen all sight from me.

Floating alone,
Lost within the ocean foam,
Can't find my way back to my home,
'Cause the deep, the depth, hides the road.

But never will I stop seeking
The things that I am believing,
Jesus giving my life and soul meaning,
Holding my hand, I know that He will save me.

I can't see the future, but be sure I know
Jesus will carry me, along with all my load,
I'll be left to tend my earthly wounds,
Wrapping them in Jesus' love so true.

Treading water now and steady,
Christ with my life jacket at the ready,
Teaching me it's mine to stir, to live my life,
No falling in the deep dark depths . . . no fall for me tonight!

Amen.

**Artwork for the poem
"Depths".**

SATAN'S THRONE

Satan sits high atop his seat, that he has declared a throne,
Snickering, speeding tattered wings, at the misery of our Earthly home.

He smiles and rubs his horns, watching His virus take mortal man,
He laughs out loud in victory, brings down a ruling hand . . .

"I shall unleash the dingy darkness,
To enslave Mother Nature to my will,
This world will fall to never-before-seen chaos,
Those left alive my virus will kill".

Content in his evil plan,
Satan spits fire on to the soul of man,
And pushes heavy on our fragile Earth,
With his dark and evil hand.

He smiles, happy with himself,
And the seeming absence of God's return?
"I will enslave the mortals", he sniggers,
"Every one of them shall burn"!

So . . . a conceited, self-proclaimed king,
Settles on his self-proclaimed throne,
The fiery doors of hell, open and swell,
As another lost Soul finds his way home.
The soul seems sunken in sadness,
This makes the Devil grin,
His head hooded and held down,
As Lucifer calls him in . . .

"Fragile creature", Satan started,
"I taste the waste upon your soul,
Welcome to an eternity my child, of hellfire and turmoil.
I will cause you suffering that you can't possibly comprehend,
This pain is endless my dear child, from here there is no end".

With an evil laugh the Devil settles,
And the soul takes down the hood, showing his eyes . . .
The Devil shivered, cold and frightened,
When he saw this soul was JESUS CHRIST!

"Hello, brother, remember me?
I'm here to help you grow,
You're getting out of hand lately,
Father and I are still trying to save your soul".

The Devil stood up quickly,
And backed up in surprise . . .
Thinking he was weaking a soul,
Then finding Mighty Jesus' eyes.

"Father? Hmmm, what's that to me? He cast me away . . .
I have no loyalty to Heaven, so, brother take yourself away!"

"Listen to me, Lucifer, we will not let you tear this world down,
Our Father sent me down to you, so we could work this out".

"FATHER? MAYBE YOURS, NOT MINE! I reject Our Fathers grace!
And I will fall this world! And then The "Father" I'll replace!"

"Oh brother, " Jesus sobbed sadly, "If that is your decree,
You will forever face,
Heavenly embrace,
Brought by The Father and from me.
You can taunt Mother Nature,
And force her to release her rage,
But we will keep Dad's children safe,
Within our Fathers Holy cage.

You can possess the one man,
And make him follow a shadowy path,
But in the end, he is forgiven -
Heaven still within his grasp.

You can send your Virus, to decay and drain all of the whole,
But we will teach them in times of trials to the Heavens you let go.
You can try to tear mortals apart, but we will preach unity,
And slicing through your shadows we will teach them family.
You can cause war and hardships, disease and misery,
But, brother, please see, that dad and me, will antidote your evil scheme.
You have no hold on victory Brother, your battle is already lost,
Dad loves His children endlessly, without a thought of cost,
And I am Father's general,
You, brother, bear in mind,
If you don't back off your antics . . .
It's my wrath you will find".

Satan stood behind his throne, scared, dumbfounded, all alone,
He tried to talk, but his lips were sewn,
He watched as The Christ turned around to go.

The Devil sits and cries,
On his self-built, self-proclaimed seat of power,
Knowing he still resides under our Father God,
Silent . . .
And still he cowers!

AMEN.

BROKEN WINGS

Can I fly on broken wings?
Can broken wings pick up a soul?
I've used tape and glue and many things
To make my broken wings become whole . . .

STILL TATTERED.
STILL BATTERED.

So, I practice and I try,
With broken wings I try to fly,
Still failing to leave ground,
As the darkness seeps in all around.

IT THINKS IT BEAT ME . . .
IT CANNOT DEFEAT ME!

I saw the shadows play,
Swift of foot, I moved away,
Then I ran and tried to fly,
Broken wings waving to the night . . .

I TOOK FLIGHT,
ON TWO BROKEN WINGS TONIGHT!

IT'S TRUE,
I FLEW!

My broken wings they weathered,
As if never, ever broke before,
I soared through the skies on broke wings
I once thought to be torn!

YOU CAN STILL FLY THE EVERYTHING,
EVEN ON A PAIR OF BROKEN WINGS!

CHAIN OF LIFE *

Every time our mighty God, creates a brand-new form from clay,
When He imparts a soul unto it and then sends it on its way,
New soul-filled clay descends to Earth,
New life falling, like feathered rain,
Constructing the first vital link
In their very own life's chain.

Every soul born from clay to life
Must carry their own chain,
Another link forged from fire and experience,
Each and every new day.

So, each day, the chain grows longer, heavier, harder to drag along,
Hell, my own chain's already over seventeen thousand chain links long!
Each link uniquely forged through trials, memories, dreams, and pain,
Each link a vital resource for you, and no two links are the same.

When the chains weight overwhelms,
Draw your power from the chain itself,
Drawing strength and wisdom through experience
Trapped in each link you've built.

So as the chain grows heavier, longer,
And starts catching on the earth,
You gain strength and you earn wisdom,
Through each link you've built since birth.
Enough to best the friction,
And force your chain to follow you,
Moving cold steel up the hill of life,
Each footstep strong and true.

There will come a day in life, however,
When you can no longer lift your chain,
It serpentines on top of you,
Trapped beneath its links in pain.

You're terrified, in agony,
Drowning within the links of your own life,
Eyes close in prayer of acceptance,
Suddenly the chain is not so tight . . .

One by one the links dissolve around you,
As your life-chain is stripped to bone,
And a warmth you've felt just once before,
Surrounds to carry your soul home.

So, as you're walking up the hill of life,
As age will make us do,
Tugging, pulling, struggling,
Dragging your chain of life with you,
Remember it's the trials, pain, and struggles
That make you what you are inside,
By persevering through your chain of life,
You return to our Lord Jesus Christ.

Praise be . . .
The chain of life and Christ grows in me . . . ALL GLORY BE!

Artwork for the poem
"Chain Of Life".

GOD'S PINOCCHIO

My whole life has been a wicked, wild, whirl-wind,
Braking before the bend, wrought and wreaked with sin!

Puppet tied to evil strings,
Made to do such evil things,
Hurting, despite objecting themes,
Beating and forced into my means.

THAT'S NO EXCUSE!
THIS PUPPET FROM EVIL WILL CUT LOOSE . . .

I'll swing a sword to twine,
Take back the life that's mine,
Immediately giving that life to Christ,
For Him to hold me safe and tight.

Then I'll smirk at the Devil,
I'll wink at evil, and bid goodbye,
I'm no longer lost within your labyrinth,
No longer twisted by your lies.

Jesus holds my hand now,
And I'm not letting go,
NO LONGER SATAN'S PUPPET . . .
NOW I'M GOD'S PINOCCHIO!

LOST

I can't breathe, and I cannot feel,
Lost between the lies and real,
I can't tell, I cannot see,
The evilness surrounding me.
I can't decipher or decode
This weighted, heavy, wicked load,
It's such a solemn, desolate road,
A lifetime being pulled and towed.

Give up? Not my vocabulary!
I shall slay this wicked beast,
I shall take its naked flesh
And upon it I shall feast.

I cannot fail, it's not possible,
I shall win, all glory be,
Right now it just seems dark,
But the darkness CANNOT take me !

KEEP THE FIGHT PEEPS!

THE CROSS *

When the darkness is upon me,
When the shadows blind my sight,
When I'm treading water in the empty,
When black fire is burning bright,
When the winds of chaos circle me
And I can only feel lost,
It is at these times of need and trials
That I LOOK TO THE CROSS . . .

When I am happy and I'm vibrant,
And my world is at peace,
When I find myself swimming in love,
And on family I feast,
When my universe is centred,
And all things are serene,
It is at these times I gaze to the cross
And Savior, bending knee.
When I'm asked about my faith,
When I'm asked how I believe,
When those questions are presented,
I reply gleefully . . .
My belief is granite,
My faith is given without cost,
When asked "How can I find peace like that?"
I simply say . . . "LOOK TO THE CROSS"!

AMEN

**Artwork for the poem
"The Cross".**

BATTLE FOR ETERNITY

"Ladies and gentlemen, kindly take your seats,
In this corner we have a man, broken in defeat,
In the other corner we have Satan, alive seven demons deep!

The challenger stands five-foot something, head held down low,
Weighing in with countless tons of sin, he's fighting to let them go.

In the Red corner, The Dark Angel, he is weightless 'though filled with sin,
And has the beckon of his dark minions to come and fight for him.

And in the white corner, a soldier of God, who freely gave to Christ His life,
And in His corner coaching him . . . the one and only Jesus Christ.

This fight has been hyped like no other before,
A mortal soul challenging the very bells of hell-fires door,
Don't look away! Don't blink, and kindly take your seat,
This is the battle for eternity, a grand memory to keep,

So . . . LET'S GET READY TO RUMMMMBBBBBLLLLLEEEE"!

ROUND 1 -

A left, a right, hitting some . . . but mostly dodging what's to come,
Left and right avoiding some, but to the chin those evil throws come.

Satan sniggers and shows his teeth, throwing a left hook at me,
Distracted I take the hit and I wobbled, but I did not bend a knee.
I threw back at Satan, but his demons intercept my vicious hit,
He looks at me with a crooked smile, as the round ending bell is hit.

ROUND 2 -

Confident and strong, I know that I can forever weather,
Still dodging and fighting, starting to see the battlefield better.

The Devil tries to draw me in, but I won't fall for that,
I fade in like I am going to, and then I unleash my Holy attack.

I swing with Holy might to my opponent's chin and it staggers the Devil back,
The Devil flicks his forked tongue at me, and throws his own wicked haymaker back.
He connected . . . I went down and kissed the caves for a time,
Jesus in my corner screaming: "Michael, you pick yourself up, remember child, you are mine"!

ROUND 3 -
Tired now, I'm weary, from the darkness fury,
Losing sight, becoming blurry, but I will keep the journey.
I will weather whatever this hellfire can bring,
There is no give up, no quit in me.

Satan is breathing heavy now, but comes straight out with rage,
A bombardment of punishment, fists flying each and every way,
I'm blocking and I'm dodging, growing tired but not throwing back,
I'll weather this shadowy storm, letting evil tire in its attack.

ROUND 4 -
Now the will of evil is tired, spent all of its energy wild,
Now is my time to strike back, telling evil I am Jesus' child.

Jab, jab, uppercut, the darkness eats it all,
I back the shadows to the ropes, and I unleash my all,
The blackness tries to strike back, but Satan has nothing left inside,
The bell rings to save him, to our corners we reside.

ROUND 5 -
Both tired now, both spent and beat,
But for me there shall be no defeat!
I'll stand up with HIM on my own two feet,
And knock all demons down, to the hard cold street,
And Satan himself in defeat,
Will bow down to me, at my very feet!

Satan comes out desperate . . .
He didn't get a good respite,
And I come forward confident,
To destroy all the shadows think they have left.

Satan heaves a heavy haymaker and catches me off my guard,
I fall back and stagger and he hits me again hard,
Seeing only stars and seeing angels, not seeing what's in front of me,
Another left, another right, I fall . . . dazed and dizzy off my feet.
Satan stands above,
Just tapping together his two gloves.
Gloating, laughing over me,
As the down count proceeds . . .

"1 . . . 2 . . . 3 . . ."
I find a holy strength inside of me . . .

"4 . . . 5 . . . 6 . . ."
To knees now and I pray, knowing I am with Jesus . . .

"7 . . . 8 . . . 9 . . ."
On my feet again with holy fire,
Satan now your mine!

The Devil did not know what to do,
As through me, the Holy Spirit flew,
He took hits and damage no one should take,
Then realized he was about to break.
And with love in heart, faith in soul, and Jesus guiding me,
I threw that one last uppercut that brought the Devil to his knees.

The count goes to completion,
Evil cowers to the light,
I stand, having beating my temptation,
Champion of God tonight.

Brought into the centre of the ring, wrist grabbed and hand held up,
Jesus right there next to me saying: "I'm proud of you my son"!

The announcer starts, "Here's your winner! What a fight!
What wonders tonight our eyes did see . . .

LADIES AND GENTLEMAN, YOUR WINNER AND TRUE WARRIOR IS
ANY SOUL ON EARTH THAT IN CHRIST TRULY, HONESTLY BELIEVES"!
AMEN.

CRACKED

Broken into pieces, the cracks in me run deep,
Staggering and stumbling on to cracked and broken feet,
I try to fill the cracks with spackle, but the putty, just won't keep,
Eyes red and burning from the tears released through the cracks in me.
Ok, I work in medical, give me sutures I'll sew the leak,
Nope . . . ain't no thread strong enough to suture cracks in me.
Once I was strong like granite, not a crack amongst debris,
Once my soul was happy, now the laughter has left me.
Every piece of me is cracked,
How can I replace what's falling out of me?
Prayer has been sent, tears have been shed,
The world's seen a "broken" me.
Breathe, just breathe, clear the mind Mike, try to see,
This is a trial . . . be it a heavy one, and through trials we release!
This hurt will haunt me, always,
Because they're embedded in the cracks in me,
But through prayer, Scripture, family, and friends,
I will seal these cracks in me!

PRAY TM (Pray To Me) *

Driving highway 66 at 3:16 am,
Gas gauge showing near empty . . . sign says gas ahead,
Stomach growling, rumbling, as I pull up to the pump,
Sign in the window says "We sell food and junk"!

Check the wallet for the funds . . . humm? . . . seems the funds are rare . . .
Another sign in the window says a " PrayTM" is there.
A.T.M. I figure and my ass is in need of cash,
So I enter the store to hit it,
No more questions asked.

Nowhere to put my card in,
The screen says "Touch me with your soul"!
I pause a minute, dumbfounded . . .
Where does my soul go?
In an instant the screen changes,
"Soul Confirmed!" is what it reads,
"Great"! I'm thinking,
Finally, I'll get the cash I need.

Nope - cash not dispensed to me, still monetarily poor,
Yet, what I got from this "PrayTM" means infinitely more! . . .

It asked of me what haunts me, and about my life's trials,
At first I was sceptical, cowered, hide, and shallow,
The "PrayTM" digs deep down at me,
I cave and let my soul fly free.
It was an ear that listened,
Support I felt deep in my heart,
It was the voice I needed,
To even find myself a start.

The "PrayTM" just gives to you,
Asking nothing of you in return,
There is no "What can you do for me?"

Nothing from me did it yearn,
I learned "PrayTM's" are everywhere!
Feeling stressed? Just hit the brakes,
Stop and find your own "PrayTM",
It's there! Make no mistake!

They're on every street corner -
One in each convenience store,
At your house . . . in your car . . .
At church there's even more!

I could not be here today without that stop on route 66,
When my life was out of gas . . .
That "PrayTM" and God gave me the fix!

P.S. John 3:16 . . . "For God so loved the world that he gave his one begotten Son, that whosoever believes in him shall never perish, but have eternal life".

Artwork for the poem
"Pray TM".

THE AFTERNOW

Each night I digest Scripture,
Each night I bend knee to pray,
I give money to the man on the street corner,
I help heal the sick by day,
I preach His word to you all –
The bad, the good, the truth,
I struggle to make up for a lost
And battered, broken youth.

This is how I will reach the Afternow -
Under HIS wing, under HIS crown.
I PRAY AND YEARN FOR THE AFTERNOW!

I've already shredded my heathen ways,
Knees bent to Jesus in endless praise,
I have shed my hate, filled it with love,
I'm changing heathen ways.
Born a rebel, always fighting,
Grown into a warrior for Jesus Christ,
Born evil and born rotten,
Made whole by the Holy light.

This is how I will reach the Afternow -
Under HIS wing, under HIS crown,
I PRAY AND YEARN FOR THE AFTERNOW.

A man of God now, and I'm brave,
My soul touched by Christ, and I've been saved,
I really see no other way,
Than bowing before HIM, screaming praise!

This is how I will reach the Afternow –
Loving all life, best I know how.
JESUS WILL GUIDE ME TO THE AFTERNOW!

PARADISE

Down for the night . . . exhausted . . . just starting to snore,
When I hear a rap . . . there it is again, lightly, upon my door.
I answer to find Jesus Christ, "Please take my hand my son!
It's time that your soul breathes free, and your new life has begun".

Climbing the stairs in a herd of tons, looking just like me,
Step by step we ascend, with Jesus Christ at the lead,
Soon we approach a mighty gate - golden laced in majesty,
With a keeper asking each of us: "What sins do you set free?"

As each of us profess, Jesus absorbs our last of sin,
And magically the golden gates open,
And saved souls start flowing in.

I can't quite explain the feeling . . . it's like suffering just dies!
The pain, the anxiety, the darkness, can't live, they can't survive.

We are brought into a grand hall, trumpets raise, so do eyes,
A scroll is opened, and a man with wings, reads to us what's inscribed . . .

We are told we are all worthy and loved,
By the one true and only Lord,
And not to cover up our eyes,
We've earned the right, through life, to view our Lord.
Then before us all
Stood what I could only call
Pure warmth and pure glory,
And a wave, like liquid love,
Washed over us,
Rushing fast and flowing free.

Then a bright flash of comfort and care,
And blinding, brilliant light,
And we found ourselves in Eden,
Starting our eternal lives in paradise.

THE DARK *

Once you're hit . . . heart blown apart . . . victim of the vile Dark,
When time stops . . . does not restart . . . held in place by dire Dark.

When things look good then fall apart, sitting wondering, where did that start?
Retracing steps finish 'til start . . . just to find out it was The Dark.

So, you post . . . you posture . . . show your meddle, show you're man,
Until The Dark with jaws wide open, devours all the land.

Swimming in the shadows, pin-point light, that might be land,
Swimming stationary . . . stuck . . . in a deep and Dark quicksand.
Can't walk it and can't swim it, time to try to fly The Dark,
Stand up tall, spread your wings, breathe in and take your arch.
Inches off the pavement, The Dark pulls violent back on you,
What other way is there to leave? Now what do you do?

You look above.
You look to love.
You look to the voice that guides you,
Sounding like a cooing dove.

You look to love, for the spark,
The spark to start the fire
To breathe Christ into the heart of Dark.
It's time to start,
To kill The Dark!
AMEN

Artwork for the poem
"The Dark".

FREIGHT TRAIN

Runaway freight train . . . I cannot apply the brakes,
Drowning in my swirly brain, sanity about to break,
Thoughts-tornado, twisting, twirling, I fall dizzy from the spin,
Battle weary, bashed and broken, unwillingly ready to give in.

I can feel my sanity cracking, I hear its pieces fracture away,
My hands tremble for no reason, caused by this freight train in my brain,
Cannot comprehend the world around me, so much I just can't understand,
Longing for release from pain, feeling like a lost soul damned!

As I give up on that cliffside, staring blankly to the ocean,
Mind filled with a thick dark fog, I'm void of all emotion,
A broken man runs towards the edge, determined to take the leap,
When a rush of warm and Holy wind, knocked me right of my feet.

"Child" I heard a loving voice chant, "Why do you dismiss your life?
Your soul is a precious gift my child, do not take this light,
This world can throw daggers, and the darkness can drip deep,
But know my child you are not alone, you stand with me beneath my wing.

We will brave this life together child, as a father and his son,
And we will stop the freight train in your brain before more damage is done,
I will melt your shadows my child, I'll pierce your blackness with my light,
Believe in yourself, love, and me once more and I will heal your life".

The voice faded, the tears fell, the freight train slowed its roll,
The fog started to dissipate, my angst was letting go,
I staggered to my feet, and shook my head to clear my foggy brain,
When I heard Jesus' voice once more saying . . . .
"Remember, always, my child . . . . our love is an unstoppable freight train!"

AMEN

IN THE MIRROR

Within the midnight mirror blackness,
Two reddened eyes beckon a stare,
Two wet, burning eyes of sorrow,
Fixed eyes to glass through cold night air.
Unaware of the sorrow's origin,
Beaten like a slave, he bears the pain,
Shackled day after day, like a prisoner,
To the shadows swamping his brain.

Swimming valiant in the quicksand,
Struggling feeble against defeat,
Each attempt to leave the sorrow
Pulls down another fifty feet.
Then one night in the mirror,
The eyes staring back weren't his,
They were bright and warming, caring eyes,
Slicing through the shadow thick.

He felt a strength about him,
The blackness of sadness fading grey,
He felt a light within his soul,
Pushing the dark sorrow far away.
Eye to glass again, and once more they're his,
Within them answers clear,
Sorrow lives and breeds within the darkness,
And dies when light is near.

Looking to Heaven teary-eyed, smiling,
"Thank you Lord for the sign!"
"Jesus' eyes staring back at me from the mirror,
When they should have been mine".
"Now when I look to my eyes within the mirror,
I will see HIS eyes inside,
I'll remember happiness is stronger then sorrow,
And sadness cannot hide".

Standing out of prayer, now happy,
He shakes his head . . . he dries his eyes,
For now he knows the secrets of the sorrow,
And has his Savior at his side . . .

It will never be as clear,
As when you see HIM in the mirror!!

BLESSINGS *

A BLESSING is not a token gift, to be received then thrown away,
A BLESSING is not a bill, that you somehow found the funds to pay,
A BLESSING is not prayer of "Please God, give me a great day"!
A BLESSING is far MORE than that, it's the way our God conveys.
A BLESSING is just that - a BLESSING, a touch from the hand of Christ,
BLESSINGS converge where they are needed, only when the time is right.
Through time and the history books, we've seen BLESSINGS abound,
But through school, and society, we dim those BLESSINGS down!
That's wrong I tell you . . . criminal, we should let and expect BLESSINGS run free,
But, that just doesn't happen, in this world of you and me.
Here's a thought, now hear me out, BLESSINGS can mend this crack,
If you give BLESSINGS to some stranger, and that someone sends BLESSINGS back.
Like a divine rain, BLESSINGS would fall, not just on one, but everyone,
It's up to us to BLESS each other . . .
"GOD BLESS YOU!" . . . there, it's begun!

Now, keep the thunder rolling, and bless another soul,
The world we're in is crumbling, but we can't just let it go!
God bless you . . . now see it through, in the name of Jesus Christ.

AMEN.

Artwork for the poem
"Blessings".

THE STORM

Rain is falling sideways, drenching already sin-soaked skin,
Wind blowing against my naked body, a cold starts from within,
Ice crystals form upon my soul from the freezing rain,
Hail shoots out of the sky, striking flesh with pain.

The snow is growing deeper, getting harder to keep my feet,
Slipping and sliding on the icy ground I find everywhere beneath me,
The tidal wave is rising up, the hurricane gains strength at sea,
Tornadoes twisting all my life, its dark winds whipping me.

The burning heat of desert sun, threatens to melt my faith make me undone,
No shelter, no cover, nowhere to run, I look to Heaven – to The Holy Son . . .

"Lord, why has this storm chased me, all my life without rest?
Storm after storm relentless, pounding hard upon my chest,
From one storm to another, blizzards to acid rain,
Why have you forsaken me, given to me all this pain"?

Then came the calm, as the storm subsided and moved along,
And I received my answer from a voice soothing, warm and calm,
"Child, hear me, I know the storms are there, they are to help strengthen you,
Every drop of rain is a trial, the wind is burden blowing through.

A pure soul cannot be handed to you, child, you must work to earn your soul,
The storm teaches you the lessons you need, to help you find that road,
Child, I know you feel you have bore suffering since the very day that you were born
But, please realize, in paradise, you'll find it was my love that grew all your storms"!

BROKEN ROAD

I have found myself walking, down a shattered broken road,
Littered with shards of serenity and contentment, sadness and sorrow,
Each new step is to unstable pavement, each new stride a brand new ride,
Earth giving out beneath me, fear of "The Fall" inside . . .

This ripped up road 'though, is the only path my life allows of me to see,
So, I start down that broken road, at each corner bending knee.
It's up to me to take on the travel, this broken road was built by me,
Every shattered brick of suffering, every jagged, broken piece.

So, stepping on emotions, to keep my head above debris,
I walk down my broken road, praying Jesus walks that road with me!

WINGS

If I had wings, I would fly
Far beyond this world, past clouds, through sky,
Until I reached Heaven, stood eye to eye
With Father God . . . Son at His side.
I'd fall in worship to the Holy right,
Drop right there, curbing my sight.

I would halt flight, and fold my wings,
Bow my head and bend my knees,
Mind racing with such random things,
Filled with the love that Jesus brings.
If only I had wings . . .
I could see such things . . .
But I must earn my wings . . .
By living with Christ inside of me.

So, I'll count the minutes passing me,
I'll spread His word, "ALL GLORY BE"!
And when He deems the time pristine,
Jesus Himself will grant me wings!

WATERFALL *

Whether you believe in God, or have no God to claim,
Whether you believe in righteousness and Jesus' Holy name,
Whatever Faith is scripture to you, there are one of two paths to claim . . .

Heed Jesus' Call,
Or
Go down the waterfall . . .

He will snatch you from the rapids, and warm your cold soul deep,
He will wrap His wings around you, He will back up shadows to defeat,
He will take your hand, and hold it, He will touch you with His grace,
The waterfall is an obstacle, that Jesus Christ can beat.

HEED JESUS CALL,
OR
GO DOWN THE WATERFALL!

At the bottom of the falls, only lies black burning fire,
The end of all desire,
Makes you cave and cower,
The waterfall is not the answer.

The answer is the Son, the answer is HIS way,
The answer is drop knee, to Jesus Christ and praise.
The answer is out there, you just need to give your all,
And Jesus Christ will rescue you, from the Hellfire waterfall!

Artwork for the poem
"Waterfall".

THE VOICE

A broken man, with broken dreams stands starring at the sea,
Crumbling rock surfing the cliffside, sadness causing him to lean . . .

Then . . . THE VOICE . . .

No one around to hear it, just a broken man, with broken dreams,
But it had to be real right? That voice that brought him to his knees!

And said . . .

"My child I know your hurting, your burden bears heavy on your soul,
Yet, is the life I gave as gift to you, such that you will let it go?
Breathe in my child and shelter here beneath your Father's wing,
Spill your sins and scars give everything to ME.
Cleanse yourself of worry, bathe in love instead,
Let my warmth surround you, let it grow and let it spread,
Now go my son, face the world, and face it holding tight onto my hand,
Face it knowing I am with always . . . I am EVERYWHERE you stand"!

And, in a tick, that was it! The voice faded away . . .
A tearful man left on his knees, then himself started to pray . . .

"My Lord Thank you for the gift, thank you for the voice,
Thank you for saving your servant from a devastating choice!
I DO feel you around me, and a warmth that I call love,
I feel your hand in mine, sense your eye watching above.
I WILL stand up and stand up proud,
I'll face the world and scream out loud -
'Sin and sadness CAN'T keep me down'!
I once was lost but now I'm found,
THANK YOU, JESUS . . . AMEN".

What was once a broken man, now whole with Jesus in his heart,
Up off his knees, and off the cliff, craving new life . . . a brand-new start,

A broken man, puzzled piece by piece, back together, because he made the choice,
To trust in God and Jesus Christ, and he listened to the voice.

DIG

Covered in clay and sweat, I must continue to dig,
Throwing soil aside, to bury the life I'm ashamed I used to live.
Making progress, the hole is deepening, breaking earth down into dust,
Digging without pause, to put to rest a soul once lost.

Digging fast and frantic, needing to get this grave six-feet,
Throw my old soul deep into it, cover it beneath my feet,
I'll then pack down the top-soil, and seal it in concrete,
Forever forgetting the heathen me, bowing at my Lord Jesus' feet.

I can't take back my past, can only beg forgiveness for what I did,
So, until I touch salvation, I will forever dig!

RELEASE *

Defeated.
Help is needed.
Soul is starving . . . need to feed it.
Can't see . . . sight is bleeding,
Blind to find the meaning.
The search seems so self-defeating,
The shadows feast . . . on me they're feeding.

Broken, torn apart,
Where did this sorrow start?
Once a man who had a heart,
A Heart swallowed by the dark,
Nothing left, not a spark,
Just burning pieces of broken heart,
Shadows dining on every part.

Time to gaze above,
To piece that heart together with love.
You know the love I'm speaking of . . .
That bright love burning high above,
The Savior . . . The Light . . . The Chosen Son.
By thy will all will be done,
Always to soldier never run.

HE will release the hurt from me,
Through Him wash sin from my feet,
He will bathe me, He will save me,
Held warm and safe under His wing.
No more shadows, now at peace,
No more darkness stalking me,
Thank you, Jesus, with ALL my love,
For giving me . . . RELEASE!

Artwork for the poem
"Release".

SEVEN NAILS

There are seven nails in this man's coffin,
Each hammered in by life and pain,
The first nail sunk deep in the day
This man dismissed dear Jesus' name.

The second nail fell when this man praised,
"I'm God in my own land"!
Lost and empty youth, running fast
And frantic from the Son of Man.

The third nail was forged by a young adult,
Who thought he owned his life,
With that also came the fourth nail,
And deep lessons taught to him tonight.

The fifth nail inched in gingerly,
As the coffin lid started to stick closed,
And a man once an enemy of God,
Realized the truth, and to The Son he rose.

The sixth nail was placed by the man himself,
To remind him of all his Sin,
To always be a bright beacon,
Thankful he was wise enough to let the true TRUTH in.

I'm sure, by now that you all have seen,
That, "This one man" That I speak of is me.
I have only one single nail left,
To be content and proud of the life I lead.

So each day I hold the nail,
Tight, between two praying hands,
And thank Jesus Christ, the carpenter,
For helping me to understand.

For HE has constructed my coffin,
And HE has driven most the nails deep into Holy wood,
But through love HE Gave the seventh nail
To His Child and that love is faithfully understood.

AMEN.

A TIRED OLD MAN

Like a blind man walking water, an aging man walks the unknown,
    A feeble man, and frightened, he must walk this road alone.
For years he felt it coming, he knew this day was stalking him,
    For years he knew that it was true, for years he did not sin.

He heard soft voices sent from Heaven, voices heard by just his ear,
    Soft warm voices of comfort, that whispered "Do not fear"!
Now this weary man lies trembling, afraid to close his eyes,
    Feeling elephants upon his chest, breath now just struggling sighs.

His thought frenzied, fast and frantic, eyes held wide, they mustn't close,
    Yet, His eyelids are so heavy, and the lust for sleep it grows,
A soft white light of comfort, tells his eyes they mustn't see,
    A voice the same as Heaven says, "Let your soul be free"!

His chronic pain is numbing now, eyelids so heavy they just fell,
    A chill of something Holy raced through his fragile dying shell,
Another whisper from the angels, finds his ears . . . an old man cries,
    As the warming voice of God commands "Please claim your wings and fly"!

An old man, oh so tired now, ends his fight to stay alive,
    An old man alone and empty see his life flash by his eyes . . .
First he sees himself an infant, tears falling now as then they fell,
    Remembering his mother's love and feeling it as well.

He sees his mother's warming smile, and gasps out "I love you"!
He relives the whole of childhood, tears dropping completely through.
He hears a familiar voice say "I do" . . . remembers man and wife,
    Weakened for an instant, an old man struggles to save life.

Proud and watching through happy tears, reliving his son born,
    But the visions changing fast and frantic, an old man's heart is torn,
Countless sights and dreams lashing out, melting together memories,
    Even thoughts lost long forgotten becoming part of what he sees.

A violent shock shot through his body, the sleep now too intense to fight,
His mind and vision blackened, after a lifetime full of sight,
Afraid but also curious, he stretches shaky hand towards light.
A tired old man ready to sleep after reliving eighty years in just one night.

He hits the light with frantic thunder, embracing sights that none have seen,
At last the riddle is clear, the end of life begins the dream.
Upon his cloud he now sits proud, sporting his silken wings,
Watching his kin and guiding them through the all of everything.

No more pain and no discomfort, he feels complete in heart and soul,
Forever protected by the paradise and love of his new home,
With a sigh, he stands and stretches . . . silken wings spread set to fly,
The old man had just discovered you live within dreams when you die.
Now, he flies!

THE CALL

I remember, deep back in the day,
Back when I thought I knew it all,
I heard something somewhere about something
I think they called "The Call" . . .

Dismissed by this heathen, but buried in his mind,
Was this "Call" important . . . a treasure left behind?

Heathens do not fret these things,
This heathen stood up tall,
Year after year bombarded with this talk about "The Call".

I grew and raised a family, blocking out it all,
All this foolish, crazy, nonsense of this thing they call, "The Call"!

Well . . . It took forty-eight years to hear it,
BUT NOW I'VE HEARD IT ALL!
It's beautiful and vibrant - the sweet sing of "The Call".

It wraps you tight in love,
Begs of you to take HIS all,
Now I sit, silent and happy,
Listening to the voice that is "The Call".

I'm just one of everyone and not a voice at all,
But I've heard it and I've heeded it,
Now I need to spread "The Call".

Gonna try to open-up those phone lines,
So HE can reach you all!
After that it's up to you to answer,
So that you don't miss "The Call".

YOU HEAL ME *

Lord, all the things that I can't see,
All the sins that are burning me,
Through all my former disbelief,
You still love and heal me!

Even when I call astray,
You still wash all my sins away,
And hold me so I know it's O.K.
You heal me in every way.

When shadows swarm, and I can't see,
You grant your glorious light unto me,
You offer shelter from the wicked dreams,
And in doing so you heal me!

No words can relay,
What it is now trying to say,
Christ, with you now, in the future, every God-given day,
Because you heal me . . . YOU HEAL ME IN EVERY WAY!

Artwork for the poem
"You Heal Me".

MY DAY OF JUDGEMENT

A bright, white light surrounds me, the mist of clouds wildly whizzing by,
A soft warm embrace of comfort surrounds me from the depths of soul to mind,
As vision clears and crispens . . . I see in the distance golden gates,
Adorned with Holy visions of the Lord, carved of pearl, blessed in grace.

A man in white sits on a pedestal, wings folded, a bright halo,
Asking of me "My child, what sins do you this day let go"?
I sit dumbfounded, without answer, and then start my life-long list,
When he stops me and tells to me "Child, let your soul itself a-test"!

So, I fold my hands, stay silent, letting Saint Peter review my immortal soul,
Wondering if I did enough in mortal life to truly, honestly, atone?
Saint Peter just looks at me and drops his glasses to tip of nose,
And with a crooked smile tells me "I love when young heathens come back home"!

"It seems that all is proper and you're a child of our Lord and Christ,
Today I grant you entrance into our Lord God's paradise".
A huge mechanical "CLANK", as if chain was striking chain,
And the gates slowly swung open exposing a golden paved pathway.

Saint Peter addressed me once again, "Enter my child and leave your sin with me,
For Christ has washed you of your sin so you may enter His paradise with a soul clean".
Scared and nervous but moving forward, with each step the golden pavers turn to cloud,
No golden path left intact behind me, only one way to keep going now.

Down the pathway, to a stairway, up the stairway to the peak,
Where stands a grand cathedral, with architecture not to be believed,
Colors, and divine carvings, pillars supported by only clouds,
A glow about the structure, a red carpet flowing down.

I hear once more Saint Peter, "Child walk the carpet, go inside,
It's time to meet The Father, it's time to embrace your new life".
Sceptical, but excited, I mount the carpet for the ride,
When it starts retracting on its own, pulling me inside.

A mist masks all of vision, eyes seeing only fog and a bright light,
Heart racing with excitement, my soul filled with delight,
I hear a voice, but not out loud, it's as if it's speaking through my soul,
I can't help but hear it, to this voice I just let go.

"My Child, I love you"! This voice boomed from within my heart,
"Welcome, my son, to eternity, this is where your new life truly starts.
I ask of you to gaze upon me, through your eyes, please see your Father's love,
Don't be afraid . . . you have been saved, there is nothing left to be scared of".

All my life, The Bible's told me, man cannot look unto our Good Lord's face,
That the divine of this righteous vision, would to a mortal decimate,
"Gaze upon me child, you've earned the right through your trials in life,
Embrace me as your true Father, Child, to me, open up your eyes".

The trust I felt was overwhelming, the truest of love I've ever felt,
Slowly, I opened up my eyes and I received such a Holy wealth,
Casting eyes to the Creator, soul safe staring into His eyes,
He tells me: "Child, you have been judged. Welcome, my son, to paradise"!

Forest thicket brilliant, grand rivers crisp and clean,
Animals of every sort around me, all bound in unity.
The sights, the smells, the taste of the air, let's my soul know it's alive,
And I settle happy and content in my new life . . .
In our God's paradise.

Amen.

PERSONAL TESTIMONIES

SUZANNE NEWMAN

To be honest, I'm not sure where to start with this! Do I include my life's history, details of childhood etc.? I do have to be aware of family members who will read this and don't really feel the need to let the entire world know every single thing about me. So, all that being said, I plan to keep this fairly brief!

I was brought up in a household where God wasn't really talked about, although we did celebrate Christmas. The Lord's name was regularly used as a swear-word and on the rare occasion prayer was mentioned, I was given the impression that it was to ask for something – a bit like a Christmas list for Santa! My Grandad was an atheist most of his life, but my Nan was a believer and went to chapel every Sunday. She was a private lady and never really discussed her faith with me. I didn't go to school with anyone who had a strong religious conviction and didn't know any neighbours that went to church/synagogue/mosque etc. Due to all this, serious thoughts of God never really entered my head until I was in my late-teens, but looking back I always felt He was there – I never thought He DIDN'T exist, I just didn't think much about His existence, or what His role was and what He meant to my life personally.

When I was 18 years old, I suddenly felt like there was a huge hole inside of me. I didn't know what it could be, but quickly worked-out that it was a Spiritual need of some sort. I spent the next 18 months speaking to work colleagues and anyone else I could about their religious beliefs, in order to find the "right" religion for me to commit to. But, to my confusion and panic, I soon discovered that none of them felt right!

Then, a new lady started work at our place and she explained to me that she was a "born-again Christian". She told me what that meant and precisely what she believed in. Everything suddenly clicked into place inside of me and I knew without a single doubt that this was what I had been searching for, or rather, what God had been calling me to and I just hadn't realised! To me, this wasn't a "religion" as such, but rather a way of life, led by a belief in the triune God and being saved through trust and faith in The Lord Jesus Christ as Messiah.

This lady and her husband spent many evenings talking with me about their beliefs, answering my questions etc. Then one evening, a group of us had gone out for a meal and it ended up with me back at her house at 3a.m., kneeling on the floor in tears of repentance and happiness as I professed my faith in Jesus Christ in prayer and asked Him to come into my life. I didn't think He would, because why would HE want ME? But to my amazement, relief and sheer joy He graciously accepted my contrite heart and sent The Holy Spirit to wash over me like a warm flood from top to toe!

I left my friend's house at 6a.m. a grateful and changed person - clean, re-born, renewed, indestructible, no longer part of or afraid of this mortal world, and filled with the joy that can only come from knowing you are saved by The Lord. I wanted to shout it from the roof tops and tell the world how great God is . . . . . . .and I still do, nearly 30yrs later!

Thank you Jesus!

Well, that's how I came to God all those years ago, but a lot has happened since then! I have cared for loved-ones with Senile Dementia, had two children, suffered an ectopic pregnancy, had surgery to remove tumours, survived (against all medical odds) a rare and very aggressive cancer in 2015/16, come back from the brink of suicide and wage an ongoing battle with clinical anxiety and depression to this day. But, I have witnessed first hand during all these testing times how The Lord is with us throughout and gives us strength, stamina and wisdom when we have none left of our own. God is our comfort and light in the darkest of times . . . without fail.

The Lord prompted me to write poetry about my times of struggle two years after my cancer journey. I have found this not only cathartic for me personally, but by sharing these poems via publishing books and posting on Facebook, I can try (in some small way) to humbly encourage others who are going through similar testing times, by witnessing to God's greatness and showing how He has been there for me. I have had much positive feedback from people in this sense so far – all glory to God for that. I acknowledge I am nothing without Him and thank Him every day for all He does, not only for me, but for everyone who has been saved in The Lord Jesus Christ and have the blessed privilege to be called "children of light".

We serve a faithful and loving God indeed, who is worthy of all praise.

PERSONAL TESTIMONIES

MICHAEL GRGICH

I WAS, WELL, I'VE always said it, a HEATHEN straight up and celebrated! I lied, stole, spat and laughed in the name of Christ, He was a joke to me, a myth, and all these stupid people were running around praising this "Jesus", pathetic and laughable, (I thought). I was God to me, no other controlled or touched me, and would argue with all my strength that truth. My morals were there, I mean I didn't go outta my way to treat people badly or anything, but I was also selfishly headstrong with a "Mike first" attitude.

I have done ALOT of things I won't detail and am far from proud of, things that have not only been wrong but also hurt a great many people. And to prove my Heathen faith at the times of the events, I didn't care - didn't care who got in the way, or who got hurt . . . friends, family, I just didn't feel remorse at all. Again, I was God of my world and God was pleased!

Over time as one would expect, my religious structure (or lack there of it) broke down - Surprise right?! Every aspect of my life, my job, my house, my kids, my health, my relationship at the time, LITERALLY EVERYTHING ALL AT ONCE OVER THE COURSE OF A YEAR BEGAN RAPIDLY DECAYING.

Anger, Fear, depression, misery, emptiness, confusion, hopeless, are a few of the adjectives I would use to describe my emotional state. So, what do you do? Well, I picked up a gun . . . fingered it, hugged it, stared at it, thought of my partner, the kids, dad, sis, etc, etc . . .

Then phone rang. I looked down and see its Rick Stockman, a childhood BFF of mine I have not seen since I was 10 years old and who I'd talked to maybe two times in 38+ years! He told me he just wanted to see how I was doing, he felt he should call. Oh, did I mention, also, Rick just happens to be a pastor? And that night he introduced me to someone that from that night forward I knew would change my life . . .

Enter Jesus Christ . . . Thank you Saviour for allowing me back into your Grace, I will forever live for you, because you lived and died for me!

That night I dumped on Rick and he posted and took it like a champ, but what really moved me (aside from a random 12am phone call from a childhood BFF pastor as I'm loving on a gun), was that as I dumped a trial on him, he quoted me right back a scripture verse that eased the pain, over and over he did this, until I set the gun down, and hung up to go to sleep . . . Rick never knew I was holding the gun.

The next month or so was confession for me, after "the event" and after speaking with Rick I knew there was more to this, a deeper touch, and I felt what I can only describe as a warming, deep in my heart, a calm, a comfort.

I found myself craving it more, like a drug, but after a life opposing Him, I didn't know how to find Him. So I teased it gently out there that I might be interested in maybe, perhaps, kinda learning a tiny shred about Him . . .

Enter Tambria Roth Carter and Randy Carter . . .

Tami (Tambria) was the victim of a pretty horrific home improvement accident and had the misfortune of being a tenant at our Hospital for quite a long time and through our working relationship we became Facebook friends. This was the way Tami approached me (on Facebook) asking me to attend church with her and Randy. After several excuses from me why I couldn't, and (thank God) their persistence, and care for my soul . . . I agreed!

That first service . . . I met HIM.

Emotions and feeling swelled in me I have never seen and did not know existed . . . I felt the entire time that the church was empty and the pastor was speaking directly and only to me and I understood the message! That night I took home my complimentary Bible and started the Bible in 40 days beginner readings. I read it in 10 days and craved more. In my life outside of Christ's book I saw change, not so much with the actual trials I was dealing with, however, in my acceptance of things, how I dealt with things, reacted to things, viewed things, all calmed. It changed from anger to patience, and my view of ALL others where once was dark and dismal hatred, now was a warm glowing love. Not only could I see this change in myself, but others close to me saw it as well. Jesus had touched me, I felt His love, how could I turn back now?

AND NOW . . .

Needless to say I'm still attending the same Church to this day. My poetry has swung dramatically from dark, desolate, and evil, to almost completely God based, with better messages of faith, hope, and love.

I was baptised in the name of Jesus Christ on April 29th 2018.

In the future, I intend to walk with Christ, constantly striving to be the best man I can to His pride. I vow to love the world and all in it and to treat it as such . . . with love.

Most of all, I look forward to continuing to learn and bond with the Scriptures, God, Christ, and The Holy Spirit, and share what I discover in hopes of helping another such as myself to find Grace in Jesus Christ. AMEN.

PERSONAL TESTIMONIES

DEBRA WHELAN

I WAS BROUGHT UP in a Jewish home where the fucus was mostly on the culture and heritage. For me, there was little interest or connection to the spiritual aspect of Judaism. However, despite this, I always had an awareness of God in my life. I knew friends who believed in Jesus and recognized a radiant light He brought into their lives. However, I wondered why my parents always said He wasn't for us?

Due to circumstances that originated in my childhood, I experienced depression, low self-esteem and anxiety. Ironically, at sixteen years old, I began to suffer from severe pain that eventually became chronic. When I was a young mother, a rheumatologist diagnosed it as Fibromyalgia, a wastebasket disease that medical professionals still have little knowledge of. Only recently have I learned how seriously our immune system is affected by our thoughts and how much the resulting health of our physical body directly correlates with our emotional state.

One afternoon, I suddenly became very ill. I thought it was a severe case of the flu but the symptoms were so much more exacerbated than any virus I had ever experienced. A few days later, after going to the emergency room, I was admitted to the hospital and soon discovered it was a serious Staph infection. Antibiotics were quickly administered but weren't immediately effective. My body began shutting down but after almost a week, the medicine finally got it under control. It almost took my life and in the process, destroyed my mitral heart valve, necessitating open heart surgery in order to repair it three years later. As I underwent a scary medical procedure, one memory I have is the kindness of a nurse who wouldn't leave my side. It was around Easter time and she handed me a palm cross to hold as she held onto my other hand, while gently comforting me. I had never felt God's presence so profoundly before and it still impacts me greatly as I reflect back.

Then in 2010, the chronic pain I had dealt with since 1971 had intensified to a new level that was off the charts! Our youngest son had recently been diagnosed with Lyme disease and was being treated by a specialist. While waiting in the doctor's office and in conversation with some of the other patients, the topic of my symptoms arose and they urged me to get tested too. I followed their advice and soon learned that my test results were also positive for Lyme disease. The IV antibiotics I was being treated with, caused my pain level to skyrocket beyond anything I had previously known. I found myself reaching out to God for mercy and prayed that He would just take me already. I was not a believer yet but found myself increasingly drawn to Him in my sufferings.

It always intrigues me as I observe how God orchestrates the events of our lives. When I was attending art school in my forties, I met a woman by the name of Cynthia, who became a fast and close friend. She has always loved the Lord and would relay some of her intriguing experiences and encounters with God. She expressed her hopes that one day I would accept Christ into my life too and she loved me so much that she continued praying about it for nineteen years! My close friend, Sue and I met several years later at work. She would occasionally talk to me about the times that Jesus had comforted her through the various trials in her life. She mentioned a Christian TV preacher who she felt would have an impact on me. I tuned in and as I listened, a new world began to unfold. I sensed that Jesus Christ was reaching out to ME! Not being familiar with Him before, I gravitated towards Him. One day, emotional and physical pain had brought me to my knees. As I watched the program, I recited the prayer of salvation and accepted Jesus Christ as my personal Savior! It was as if I was thrown a lifeline. After that, I began to notice a gradual transformation . . . my outlook began to change and I viewed life through a more optimistic lens. There was an internal comfort and a renewed sense of peace about me. The pain flare-ups were still present but I sensed a Divine intervention.

In 2018, the tension and constant clenching of my jaw really escalated. It led me to seek answers regarding TMJ, caused by a misaligned bite. One thing led to another and I came upon a specialty dentist who determined it was indeed TMJ and provided a noninvasive approach to treatment. The frequency of the pain, although still unbearable when it did occur, decreased from every day/24/7 to a few times per month, which to me was a huge improvement!

Fast forward to 2020, my heart valve failed and needed replacing, so it was time to undergo a second open heart surgery. Although it was an unpleasant experience, I couldn't have done it without God. His constant presence was with me throughout and thanks to His grace and mercy, He got me through it with flying colors! Praise the Lord!

Although chronic pain has impacted me for fifty years at this writing and I've endured plenty of health and emotional trials along the way, I believe God has used them to draw me towards Him in order to build my faith! In retrospect, I probably wouldn't have sought Him, had I never experienced them. I'm humbled and honored by God's unfailing love, blessings, grace and mercy. I've come to learn that no one is too broken for God to fix and I'm a perfect example! Jesus sacrificed His life on the cross so that those who follow Him can have Life and live it abundantly and purposefully. He took our sin and bore the punishment for us! What a special gift that is, of which I'm eternally grateful to receive! I hope that my testimony has served to bless and encourage you in some way and may the light and love of God always be upon you!

STEPS

(A collaboration between Michael Grgich and Suzanne Newman)

Staring at the grand staircase,
Insurmountable it seems,
Each step leads you to Heaven,
But also has hidden traps that can't be seen.

"Steady!" I tell my own feet,
As I lift myself up one more rung,
Closer now than I ever have been,
To Heaven, and Jesus – God The Son.

But as I keep on climbing,
On several stairs I seem to fall behind,
Find myself repeatedly slipping down . . .
Gain one step, then I slide down five!

GOTTA START THESES STEPS WHILE I AM ALIVE,
FOR I HOLD INSIDE, A SPIRITUAL DRIVE.

For I can't climb celestial stairs,
When I'm already dead and gone,
For choices then come much too late –
Damned feet are on the downward rung.

And I've already dipped a toe
In Hell's fire, and was terrified,
But in God's love I've seen the light,
And so my aim is Heaven's sky.

But trials, struggles and ill health,
Make me trip up, on this staircase,
I hang on by my wobbling heels,

Supported by the Lord's good grace.

Temptation, sin and Satan
Grease the steps, to make me slip and fall,
But I stand firm in Jesus Christ,
And climb on up, towards God's call.

My shoes may wear and fall apart,
But I'll still climb with my bare soles,
For inside I am crying, dying,
Desperate for my peace-filled goal.

I KNOW I HAVE TO REACH MY DESTINATION,
SO ONWARD I CLIMB WITHOUT HESITATION . . .

Each step is built by action, deeds,
A construct of kindness, or forged from pain,
The Devil plotting, smiling, trying to strip the stairs,
As I walk this way.

Sometimes a footfall triggers traps,
And the shadows spread their evil glue,
The wicked trying to halt my climb,
And hide the Saviour, Christ, from view.

But pure eyes can pierce the darkness,
And Jesus will make Himself be seen,
So forever onward, forever upward,
I climb each step to reach the dream.

JESUS' HAND HOLDING MINE AS HE ASCENDS THESE STAIRS WITH ME,
I'M WALKING WITH THE SHEPHERD, WHO'S MY GUIDE WHEN I CAN'T SEE.

It's alright when my balance flails,
Or poor stamina means I'm weak and ail,
For Christ will lift and carry me
Towards the light, that I can see.

The Devil plots to rig each rung,
To make me fall and come undone,
He uses sorrows, trials and grief,
To make me fall to Hell beneath.

He sets his snares, creates trap-doors,
To injure, break and make me sore,
He makes the stairs seem old and rotten,
But God's with me – I'm not forgotten.

In faith, I climb and march along,
For Salvation's made me bold and strong,
And my soul wants its spiritual crown,
So I'll ascend and not look down.

It matters not if broken stairs,
Leave me just dangling, in mid-air,
For God throws me a safety-line,
Held by Jesus Christ, in love divine.

Then, one day, when my climb's complete,
I'll fall in reverence at Christ's feet,
For I will be – in God's fine grace,
Finally resting in His Heaven's place.

Written jointly by Michael Grgich (MAG) and Suzanne Newman

**Artwork for the poem
"Steps".**

www.ingramcontent.com/pod-product-compliance
Lightning Source LLC
Chambersburg PA
CBHW051942160426
43198CB00013B/2260